Dating with Purpose

Dating with Purpose

A SINGLE WOMAN'S GUIDE
TO ESCAPING NO MAN'S LAND

DR. ERICA HOLMES

Foreword by Sheryl Lee Ralph

HOMMs Hands
PUBLISHING

Published by HOMMs Hands Publishing, Los Angeles, California
www.docerica.com

Edited and designed by Girl Friday Productions
www.girlfridayproductions.com

Cover and interior design: Rachel Marek
Project management: Sara Addicott
Image credits: back cover © suns07butterfly/Shutterstock

ISBN (paperback): 978-1-7332320-0-5
ISBN (e-book): 978-1-7332320-1-2

Library of Congress Control Number: 2019908385

First edition

This book is dedicated to Mary A. Holmes (RIH) for the labor of her hands and the sharing of her heart. And to all the women who have, directly and indirectly, allowed me to share their journeys.

CONTENTS

FOREWORD

There is nothing like a shared loving relationship. My parents raised me to plan, to be assertive, and to work diligently for what I wanted in life. As a family, we lived in a home where respect, love, and high expectations were as important as breathing. Decisions were expected to be thought out, reasoned, and explainable.

My Jamaican mother and American father blended the best of both cultures to form a strong foundation for their children to succeed. It was this foundation that I would fall back on as I dealt with one of the most difficult times in my life.

My divorce put me through it. It was a dark time for me, one that conjured up feelings of inadequacy, self-doubt, and pain in ways that I had never felt before. Those thoughts impacted my health, and I understood clearly why some people turn to alcohol or drugs to cope with the pain. Nothing in my life had ever caused me to question myself so deeply.

Divorce was never in my plan—nor did I ever see myself as a divorcée—especially not with two young children. It really was a defining moment. I could see myself sinking into that sunken place. I had to make up my mind real quick: *Sheryl, are you going to sink or swim?* I chose to swim.

In that moment, I chose me. What does that mean? It means I decided that honoring me, respecting me had to be first. The decision to love and care for myself was the first step in my personal healing. Not only did I have two small children to raise, but I also had a career to keep on track. I had to sharpen my ability to deal with my life and its ups and downs. My future love life would be shaped by this moment. I could either recall the examples of love, trust, and respect I saw in my parents or stay in the sunken place. I chose me, and I was ready for the next phase of my life.

It was in this state of mind that I met and married my second husband. Learning from the past, I prioritized my needs and desires, using my ability to communicate my non-negotiables. This would prove to be important in any relationship. I knew my areas of compromise and had again formed a healthy relationship with myself. I was dating with a purpose.

Over the years, I have met so many women who have been held captive by their past and have allowed their feelings of inadequacy and shame to shape their lives and relationships with men. "Any man is better than no man" or "he's not exactly what I want, but he is not that bad" have become excuses for too many women who lack the confidence or insight to challenge themselves to think differently about who they are, what they want from their relationships, and what their motivations for pursuing love are.

Taking the time to understand who you are and what you bring to your relationships puts you in the best place to date and move forward in other areas of your life. It's foundational, ladies! Like the great drag queen RuPaul said, "If you can't love yourself, how in the hell are you going to love somebody else?"

As you prepare to start this incredible workbook, remember that honoring and respecting yourself must be first. Your respect for yourself will show him and others the starting point for engaging with you and let them know the types of actions that are off-limits. But most importantly, you will move with confidence, which really is the sexiest thing on earth!

And remember, always be true to who you are: Divinely Inspired Victoriously Anointed!

Your DIVA,
Sheryl Lee Ralph

INTRODUCTION

In its purest form, dating is auditioning for mating
(and auditioning means we may or may not get the part).

—*Joy Browne*

What are your initial thoughts and feelings when you hear the word *dating*? Do you smile with anticipation or tremble with fear? Do you dismiss it as a futile endeavor, or do you daydream about the possibilities? The word *dating* conjures up a variety of visceral reactions that are as unique as the women reading this introduction. These reactions are influenced by numerous factors. Personal history with dating, witnessing the dating successes and failures of friends, our beliefs about ourselves, our beliefs about relationships, and our beliefs about ourselves in relationships, among many other things, shape our ideas and attitudes about dating. Now follow *dating* with the word *purpose*, and many immediately form a mental picture of an exaggeratedly wide-eyed woman in tattered clothing who is frothing at the mouth and wringing her hands as she stands on a street corner looking at every man that passes by. What most women fail to realize is that you are dating with a purpose, whether you are aware of it or not.

Your behaviors signal your intentions to potential partners. Early on, your behaviors impact your ability to get a date, signal your expectations while on the date and subsequent dates, and set the foundation for the future of the relationship. Similar to your reactions to hearing the words *dating* and *purpose*, your dating behaviors are influenced by your thoughts and emotional appraisals of the situation. Simply put, your thoughts about a situation impact the way you feel, and the way you feel impacts the way you behave. I like to think of these behaviors as traffic signs that inform "potentials" of the rules of engagement. Whether you are consciously aware of it or not, you are communicating your dating purpose before you even say one word.

Unfortunately, most of us are not taught to become aware of what we are doing or why we are doing it. As a result, many of our thoughts, feelings, and behaviors automatically occur, and the motivations are outside of our conscious awareness. Once we become overwhelmed by our emotional reactions, we become driven by feelings, which can impair logical thought. This causes us to act based on what we feel—our passion—rather than to use what we know.

For example, let's say that Ruby went on a fabulous date last night. They both seemed to enjoy themselves; he even remarked that Ruby was "a breath of fresh air." As they parted for the evening, he said, "I'll call you tomorrow." As she prepared for bed the next night, she realized that it was 10:00 p.m. and he hadn't called. What was Ruby's initial thought when she realized he hadn't called? Let's say that her initial thought was *Wow, I guess he didn't like me after all.* What feelings would be associated with a thought like this one? Anger? Sadness? Shame? What behaviors might those feelings elicit? Crying? Cursing? Isolation? Resolve never to talk to him again? Now let's say that her initial thought was *My goodness, I haven't heard from him all day. I hope he's all right.* What feelings might follow that thought? Concern? Worry? Curiosity? What behaviors might those feelings elicit? Perhaps a check of his social media to see if he's been active today, or a Google search to see if there were any major accidents reported with his name mentioned, or a quick text to say, "Hi, I didn't hear from you today and I wanted to make sure that you're OK." The point of these examples is not to say that any one reaction is "better" than the other but to point out that there is no evidence to support that either of those thoughts are true. However, there are feelings associated with the (unproven) thoughts and resulting behaviors.

In reflecting on both initial thoughts above, how might the results have differed had Ruby stopped and said, "I don't know what he's thinking or what happened in his world today. The only thing that I know is that he didn't call, and I was looking forward to speaking to him. What are my options?" Had this happened, Ruby would have stopped the spiral of emotional reactions to her spontaneous thoughts and engaged in intentional thinking, leading to informed feelings, resulting in purposeful behavior. Successful dating incorporates both the head and the heart. You do not have to sacrifice one for the other to achieve what you desire.

Dating with Purpose: A Single Woman's Guide to Escaping No Man's Land is an invitation to date differently. There is no magic path to finding a mate, but there certainly are strategies and tools that can help you position yourself for success. And it all begins with you. It is only through an exploration, increased awareness, and acknowledgment of who you are in relationships that you will be able to get rid of unconscious unproductive past behaviors in favor of deliberate, thoughtful actions.

The activities in this workbook are designed to facilitate exploration of your relational self and give you practical tools to date intentionally and to increase your odds of finding the relationship you want. My goal is to move the attention away from who he is to help you discover who you are. It is only by discovering who you are in a relationship that you are able to truly understand your wants and needs, what you are willing to take and give in a relationship, and what steps you are willing to engage in to make it happen. Without this insight, your behaviors become confusing, inconsistent, and contradictory to everyone, including yourself.

This workbook is not designed to be a guide on how to learn to flirt or how to pick up guys. It will not give you information on how to make a better online dating profile or how to pick the perfect "club" outfit. Hence, the chapters that discuss specifics about dating (chapters 6, 7, and 8) are the shortest. This workbook is designed to get you prepared to date by looking in the mirror rather than out the window. Therefore, the chapters that inspire self-reflection make up the bulk of the material.

The exercises encourage you to reflect on early messages that you received about being active in dating and your role when in relationships. Further exploration of the types of relationships you saw growing up and repeated patterns is necessary to understand how you were influenced. Additionally, it is imperative to consider the type of guy you've been historically attracted to and how he compares to your values, desires, and boundaries.

The questions throughout this workbook help you transform through reflection. The bulleted points are pieces of the puzzle that, when put together, form the foundation for a holistic view of yourself in relationships and will begin to chart a pathway to dating with purpose.

Be honest with yourself. Don't begin this book if you are not ready to take responsibility for your life.

1

Dating with Purpose Versus Dating Desperation

Our need for someone to share our lives with is part of our genetic
makeup and has nothing to do with how much we love ourselves
or how fulfilled we feel on our own . . . Attachment is an integral
part of human behavior throughout the entire lifespan.

—John Bowlby

AM I DESPERATE?

As you begin to read this book, it is important that we are all on the same page. To ensure this, I will begin by clarifying the primary premise of the book. Many people confuse the idea of purposeful dating with desperation. These two concepts are very different from each other. So let's begin by looking at the definitions of both words. Purpose is defined as "having as one's intention or objective." Synonyms for purpose are words like intent, aim, plan, design, decide, resolve, determine, and aspire. Alternatively, desperation is defined as a "state of despair, typically one that results in rash or extreme behavior." Its synonyms are hopelessness, distress, anguish, agony, torment, misery, and wretchedness. As you can tell, these words don't just contrast each other but are in some ways polar opposites.

Additionally, the word purpose in this context is coupled with a verb, and as we all know, verbs are action words. Therefore, a woman who moves with purpose is not in a state of despair—she is focused on an objective. A woman who moves with purpose is not hopeless; she aspires to achieve something. A woman who moves with purpose is not distressed or anguished but is resolved and determined to make things happen rather than to passively let things happen to her. Therefore, a woman who moves with purpose does not engage in extreme or rash behavior but advances with well-planned intentions.

So why do many people confuse putting energy into finding a relationship with desperation? I would argue that, historically, women have been socialized to be the recipient of a man's advances. From a young age, girls are taught that courting gestures like being asked on a date or proposals of marriage are outside of their purview and control. This socialization essentially means to make yourself available and wait, since the rest is men's territory. Therefore, if you put energy into your availability, you are categorized as desperate, easy, a sad and lonely basket case who will never find a good man because good men want women who are waiting on the sidelines to be advanced upon.

With the advancement of feminism, many of the messages given to young girls have begun to change. The notion of the traditional female gender role has shifted significantly since the 1960s and '70s. The idea of women putting effort and energy into becoming academically successful, professionally successful, or excelling in once male-dominated arenas is part of the current zeitgeist. In 2019, these achievement-oriented behaviors are not only accepted but expected.

However, the same can't be said for dating behavior and gender expectations. Often when a woman says, "I really want to be in a relationship" or "I wish I had someone to share my life with," she is met with criticisms from her peers (with other women being some of the worst offenders). Responses can range from "You should just really learn to be happy by yourself" to "Just be patient, a relationship will come" to "Girl, I don't need a man; I've got BOB—my battery-operated boyfriend—at home." On the other hand, women are often praised for making statements like "I am perfectly fine by myself," "I have lots of things to keep me busy," or "I'm not dating anyone right now, but it's cool."

Of course, that is not to say that you shouldn't be happy in your singlehood or that you need a man to make you whole or that hobbies aren't good things to have. I am merely pointing out that if you desire a relationship, then putting energy into accomplishing that desire should be encouraged, just as going back to school to get your degree, going after that promotion, saving for a house, or getting healthy would be.

Does *any* of this sound familiar? Does it ring true in relation to your experience? Use the following exercises to reflect on your experience.

Reflection

🦋 What direct and indirect messages was I given about "desperate" women? What behaviors do they engage in? How should I feel about desperate women?

_____

_____

_____

_____

_____

_____

_____

_____

_____

_____

_____

_____

🦋   What messages was I given about dating? What messages was I given about dating with purpose? (These could have been direct or indirect messages.)

_____

_____

_____

_____

_____

_____

_____

_____

_____

_____

_____

🦋   How have those messages shaped the way that I have dated in the past? What do I do or don't do to be available to be found?

_____

_____

_____

_____

_____

_____

_____

_____

_____

_____

_____

_____

✹ What comes up for me when I think about dating with purpose? What concerns do I have about dating with purpose? What would dating with purpose "say" about me?

_____

_____

_____

_____

_____

_____

_____

_____

_____

_____

_____

_____

_____

_____

_____

_____

_____

_____

_____

_____

_____

_____

_____

_____

_____

_____

_____

_____

_____

If you are still a little leery about the distinction between dating with purpose and dating in desperation, or you don't know where you fall on the continuum, let me highlight some common thoughts and behaviors that are associated with being purposeful and being desperate. Take some time to honestly reflect on where you fit.

✸ Put an X next to each behavior that you have exhibited when dating (appendix 1).

DATING WITH PURPOSE	DATING IN DESPERATION
❑ Interested in finding a long-term relationship	❑ Change your behaviors to get him to like you
❑ Honest about needs and desires	❑ Agree with everything that he says
❑ Direct	❑ Planning your wedding mentally not long after you first meet
❑ Reflect on your role in the relationship	❑ Always available
❑ Emotionally available and stable	❑ Cancel previously made plans when he says he wants to see you
❑ Have identified and communicated dealbreakers	❑ Dig for compliments
❑ Willing to walk away if dealbreakers occur	❑ Need to be told often that he likes you
❑ Well-defined and communicated boundaries	❑ Insecurity
❑ Comfortable saying no	❑ Become anxious if you are unable to answer every time he calls
❑ Comfortable saying yes	❑ Buying gifts and giving money
❑ Dates with both head and heart	❑ Settle/lower your standards so that he fits them
❑ Takes time to get to know him	❑ Wavering boundaries
❑ Not looking for a "project"	❑ Clingy
❑ Ready for commitment	❑ Popping up at his house or job uninvited
❑ Willing to leave unhealthy relationship	

❑ Comfortable maintaining your identity when in a relationship	❑ You truly believe that a part of a man is better than no man
❑ OK with taking it slow	❑ You tell him sad stories to make it more difficult for him to leave you
❑ Comfortable allowing him to be him and you to be you	❑ Justify his rude, disrespectful, or bad behavior
❑ Not willing to settle	❑ Send long, emotional text messages
❑ Not emotionally reactive	❑ Become upset when he is unavailable
❑ Are clear about why you are dating	❑ Use sex to "help" him commit to the relationship
❑ Outline those things that you are looking for in a mate	❑ Believe that if you have sex with him, he will stay
	❑ Believe that if you have a child with him, he will stay

Review the items you checked above, and list the top three to five dating behaviors that you would like to change.

1. _____

2. _____

3. _____

4. _____

5. _____

Most women have some behaviors in both categories. However, if you have checked more behaviors in the column on the right than in the one on the left, you might be on the desperation spectrum. But don't despair—there is still time to move from desperate to purposeful. Yes, it's time to learn a new way of being in relationships. It is important when dating with purpose to know who you are, to know what you want, and to move intentionally to make that happen.

GOALS

The first step to completing the *Dating with Purpose* workbook is to define your goal. You might assume that your goal is obvious. However, desired outcomes will differ for each woman. Some women want to get married, some might want a long-term committed relationship, while others might be looking for a way to have more fun dating. Some women might want to learn some new skills to improve their dating life, and others might want to understand themselves better. Only you can determine your goal.

 Take some time and define your purpose for dating. Use these statements to spell out your goals.

I see myself being married within the next three years.	Yes	No
I think that dating someone for five or six years is just as fulfilling as a marriage.	Yes	No
I really enjoy the process of dating.	Yes	No
At the completion of this workbook I want to understand:		
At the completion of this workbook I want to know:		
At the completion of this workbook I want to do:		

Use your answers above to formulate your goal in completing this workbook.

 My dating goal is:

_____

_____

_____

_____

Guided Imagery Exercise

There is an old saying that states, "You must see it in order to be it." This exercise involves visualizing a detailed image of yourself achieving your stated dating goal. Imagery involves evoking all five senses as well as emotion. It is something we mentally feel, hear, see, smell, taste, or touch.

To begin, close your eyes and start to create an image in your mind. Imagine that you are moving confidently, dating with purpose. What would it be like if you were dating with purpose? Imagine how you would behave. How would you carry yourself? What new places would you visit? What would you say if you were dating with purpose? How would you communicate? Imagine yourself in conversation with a guy. Visualize your facial expressions, your word choice, your body language. Imagine the feelings and body sensations that you'd have. Spend some time visualizing all aspects of your image. Take some time developing the image and noticing how you show up. Spend at least fifteen minutes visualizing.

Afterward, write down what you noticed about yourself. How does your guided imagery differ from the way you currently date?

_____

_____

_____

_____

_____

_____

_____

_____

_____

_____

_____

_____

_____

_____

_____

_____

_____

_____

_____

_____

_____

_____

_____

_____

_____

_____

_____

_____

_____

_____

_____

_____

_____

_____

_____

As you move through this workbook, take time to revisit this visualization exercise. Continue to see yourself dating with purpose, being the woman you'd like to be. Notice how you feel about yourself during and after the visualization, and begin to carry those feelings with you throughout your day.

BE SMART

 What are you committed to doing from this point forward to realize your dating goal? Write down at least three SMART (specific, measurable, achievable, realistic, time-framed) behavioral actions. It is OK if you do not have more than one goal at this point. As you complete this workbook, you will learn specific tools, skills, and strategies to help you realize your goals. As you go through the chapters, feel free to add to and/or update your goals.

SPECIFIC BEHAVIORS	MEASURABLE	ACHIEVABLE	REALISTIC	TIME-FRAMED
Example: I will read the Dating With Purpose *workbook.*	*I will complete the first chapter.*	*I will work in the book for one hour per day.*	*I will work in the book at least five days a week.*	*I will complete the chapter by March 1.*

Congratulations! You have begun a new chapter in your dating life. Just by reflecting on the messages that you were given about dating and what your behaviors "say" about you, you have begun to put yourself in a position to make a conscious decision about how you date. Chapter 1 was created to help you to begin to think about your dating notions and how these notions impact your dating behaviors. By challenging these ideas, you free yourself to develop new ideas and thus to engage in new behaviors based on your new ideas. This allows you some control over how you "move." By setting goals and visualizing yourself achieving these goals, you begin to move with purpose toward making your vision a reality.

Chapter 1 Reflection

What did I learn about myself in this chapter?

_____

_____

_____

_____

_____

_____

_____

_____

_____

_____

_____

_____

_____

_____

_____

_____

_____

🦋 What did I learn about my dating habits in this chapter?

_____

_____

_____

_____

_____

_____

_____

_____

_____

_____

🦋 What do I want to change about my future dating behavior?

_____

_____

_____

_____

_____

_____

_____

_____

_____

_____

_____

_____

What skills and tools did I learn in this chapter?

_____
_____
_____
_____
_____
_____
_____
_____
_____
_____
_____
_____
_____
_____
_____
_____
_____

2

I Know Me

*If you take the same bricks from your past relationship
into your new one, you'll build the same house.*

—Unknown

IT'S REALLY A DANCE

Before attempting to cultivate a new relationship, it is important to reflect on your past relationships, their demise, and your role in their destruction. So often when relationships end, our conversations are centered on "what he did wrong." We have all spent countless hours hearing about or talking about the things that he did to hurt you, lie to you, cheat on you, not commit to you, abandon you, et cetera. But what is frequently missing from those conversations is discussion about our role in creating a dynamic that made space for those things to occur. No, I am not saying that it is your fault that he behaved "badly." However, I am saying that we must take responsibility for the dynamics of our relationships. As the common saying goes, "We teach people how to treat us."

Relationships are co-created. It is extremely difficult to be in a relationship of one. When we enter into an intimate relationship, we engage in both overt and covert behaviors that tell our partner what they can expect from us. It really is a dance. The overt behaviors are the things that we state we want, what we will and will not tolerate, and how we expect to be treated. Our covert behaviors consist of the unspoken interactions that signal to our partner our unspoken desires and limits. As you might guess, the covert behaviors are more influential in teaching our partner limits than the overt statements. For example, you say: "I won't date someone who cheats on me," but when you discover infidelity, you work it out because you've already invested twelve months in the relationship. Or "I'm really looking for a man who is available and consistent," but when he disappears for a couple of days it's OK because he had an extremely "good" explanation. Or "I don't have sex on the first date," but it happened, and you are crushed that he did not call you the next day. Tony Gaskins says, *"You teach people how to treat you by what you allow, what you stop, and what you reinforce."* At some point your expressed desires become idle talk, and your partner learns that your boundaries are weak, your standards are low, and your rope is long. Therefore, it is important to say what you mean and mean what you say. Your behavior and your words must be in alignment.

Women give varying reasons for behaving in a way that contradicts what they say they want or will not tolerate, in order to remain in a relationship that doesn't align. Three very common justifications are:

1. "I wanted to keep the relationship." Well, if you are reading this book, the relationship ended anyway and you compromised your values.
2. "By that time, I was in love with him." But did he honor, cherish, and respect your love? It is not easy to release love once you've let it in. Let's be honest. It is downright painful to let go. The pain is intensified because you not only let go of the person but you let go of the dreams for the future that were tied to him. However, giving your love to someone who does not cherish it is like putting rose petals in the toilet.
3. "He didn't mean it." OK, so what did he mean? There is a very famous quote attributed to Maya Angelou: "When people show you who they are, believe them the first time."

I've listed only three; however, there are many, many more reasons. Think about times when you did not follow through, when your words did not line up with your actions.

Reflection

Think of two instances when you've made statements about your limits, but when push came to shove, you didn't follow through. Reflect on what impacted your behavior.

🦋 Describe situation #1: What did you say? And then: What did you do?

_____

_____

_____

_____

_____

_____

_____

_____

_____

_____

_____

_____

_____

_____

_____

_____

_____

_____

🦋 Why didn't you follow through? (Be honest with yourself.)

_____

_____

_____

_____

_____

_____

_____

_____

_____

_____

_____

🦋 Describe situation #2. What did you say? And then: What did you do?

_____

_____

_____

_____

_____

_____

_____

_____

_____

_____

_____

_____

_____

🦋 Why didn't you follow through? (Be honest with yourself.)

_____

_____

_____

_____

_____

_____

_____

_____

_____

_____

_____

🦋 On a scale of 1 to 10 (1 = extremely easy and 10 = emotional death): If you were in situation #1 again, how difficult would it be for you to follow through?

1 • 2 • 3 • 4 • 5 • 6 • 7 • 8 • 9 • 10

Explain your response:

_____

_____

_____

_____

_____

_____

_____

_____

🦋 On a scale of 1 to 10 (1 = extremely easy and 10 = emotional death): If you were in situation #2 again, how difficult would it be for you to follow through?

1 • 2 • 3 • 4 • 5 • 6 • 7 • 8 • 9 • 10

Explain your response:

_____

_____

_____

_____

_____

_____

_____

_____

_____

_____

🦋 What is the likely outcome if you continue to choose not to follow through on the limits you set?

_____

_____

_____

_____

_____

_____

_____

_____

_____

_____

_____

If you have had difficulty in the past—for instance, making idle threats, blurting out things in anger, or following through when the time comes—then making the shift might be rather challenging. However, changing this behavior is imperative if you want to begin to date with purpose. There is power and purpose in the follow-through. By following through, you are honoring yourself, him, and the relationship.

Five Steps to Following Through

🧩 Stop and think before you make a declaration.

It is very easy to blurt out an ultimatum in the heat of a disagreement. It is normal to want to fire back a hurtful notice of abandonment when someone has hurt you. The real problem begins after the dust settles and you then try to take it all back or pretend that you never said it. One way to prevent this scenario is for you to learn to respond rather than react. There is a difference, you know. A reaction is typically automatic, without much thought, often quick, and tends to be aggressive. A response usually occurs sometime after the initial action and is planned, thought out, and calm. Take time after an event to think about what you really want to do and what you have the current capacity to do, and then respond. Just because something occurs, it doesn't mean that you can't take some time to pull yourself together before you address it. Once you calm down, you will be in a better place to say what you mean. Time should allow you to balance emotions and thoughts.

🧩 Be clear with yourself about what you want and what you don't.

You can never plan for every possible scenario that could arise in your relationship. What you can do is clarify your values, your relationship desires, and your dealbreakers long before you meet him. Your values and dealbreakers are not relationship dependent. They should be stable across relationships because they solely depend on you. You will have an opportunity to identify these in chapter 5. Once you have determined these, you can rely on them in order to date with confidence and develop a plan to implement them if need be. Your relationship desires can be influenced by a great guy who might provide something that you never knew you wanted, but your values and dealbreakers should be less wavering.

🧩 Make statements to communicate your boundaries, not to threaten.

Having clearly communicated boundaries is essential to holding yourself and your partner accountable for your actions as well as his. When you clearly communicate your boundaries, you allow your partner the freedom to decide whether or not they feel that they can meet your expectation. Threats are about control and cohesion. Threats communicate "Either you do what I want you to, or I will punish you." Boundaries, on the other hand, convey your limits. Boundaries communicate "This is OK with me, and this is not."

🧩 Do what you say you are going to do.

Remember that you are teaching him how to treat you. Everything that you do teaches him what you feel you deserve and what you will allow. If you do not follow through, especially with your dealbreakers, you are likely to set a precedent that is very difficult to undo.

🧩 Prepare.

One of the most important steps to following through is developing strategies for handling the follow-through. This is also probably the most difficult part, because it is the part that usually involves the potential loss of the relationship. However, it is important for you to have strategies and a plan in place so that when it happens (and it will happen), you have alternatives to going back on what you've said or going back to him. So how will you deal with the pain of the letting go? How will you deal with the pain of staying with someone who does not respect your boundaries, values, or dealbreakers?

List some things you can do to help you deal with the loss of the relationship due to your follow-through. Think of things that can help you handle the pain, longing, self-doubt, loneliness, and other thoughts and emotions that might come up during this time. Some examples: journaling, engaging in a new hobby, spending more time with friends, yoga, meditation, spiritual practices.

_____

_____

_____

_____

_____

_____

_____

_____

_____

_____

_____

_____

_____

_____

_____

_____

_____

_____

_____

_____

_____

_____

_____

_____

_____

_____

_____

Reflection

🦋 Reflect on the Five Steps to Following Through. Which step(s) do you think will be the most difficult for you to implement? Why?

_____

_____

_____

_____

_____

_____

_____

_____

_____

_____

_____

🦋 What can and will you do to develop your ability in this area?

_____

_____

_____

_____

_____

_____

_____

_____

_____

_____

_____

MY DATING NAME GAME

Continuing the journey to becoming aware of your dating behavior involves acknowledging the behavioral qualities that impact your ability to develop and sustain a healthy relationship. These are behaviors, traits, and attitudes that you are usually aware of, on some level, that you engage in during dating relationships. Most often we become aware of them because people have told us that we do them. Often we discount that feedback from others because we see it as criticism. It can be difficult for us to see those behaviors in ourselves, because we're just being us. But I am sure that you can quickly describe the relationship-interfering behaviors that your best girlfriend engages in. If asked, you probably wouldn't have to think about it for more than sixty seconds. It is important for us to be honest with ourselves and be willing to embrace ourselves, even our flaws. We might not be able to change them quickly or at all. Nevertheless, acknowledging them can go a long way to helping you understand what you do, how it might impact others, and what you need. I know that it is much easier to look at someone else and see how their behaviors interfere with dating success. Therefore, the Dating Name Game was created to help you look at your dating behaviors from the outside, as if your behaviors could stand alone. To be clear: I am not talking about an alter ego, like Beyoncé/Sasha Fierce or Diana Prince/Wonder Woman or Dr. Jekyll/Mr. Hyde. Your relational behaviors are not another side of you that comes out when you want to do something that "regular old you" would never do. Your relational behaviors are very much a part of you and surface naturally as a result of trying to be in an intimate relationship. Your relational behaviors are a patterned way of being when dating, or a theme that describes your actions in a relationship. I have listed ten examples below to help you get the idea. See if you can recognize yourself or someone you know.

MS. CONTROLLING: It's either her way or the highway. Ms. Controlling doesn't ask; she directs, instructs, demands. From her perspective, there is a right and wrong way to do nearly everything. There is a perfectionist quality to her, even though she's far from perfect. At the core of Ms. Controlling is an overwhelming fear that she will not be "taken care of" or have her needs met by anyone other than herself. Not only are her behaviors annoying but they can make her man feel inadequate, like a failure, and undervalued.

LADY DOORMAT: Famously known for responding by saying "Whatever you like." In some ways she is the opposite of Ms. Controlling. Lady Doormat has very loose boundaries, has difficulty holding her partner accountable for his behavior, and often allows him (and others) to "walk all over her." At the core of Lady Doormat are feelings of low self-esteem and of not being deserving of love and respect. Unfortunately, Lady Doormat attracts abusive men like a moth to a neon welcome sign. Although her man might not be physically abusive, he will have abusive and user traits. He will not respect the weak boundaries that she attempts to set, and he will walk all over her.

DUCHESS NEEDY: Duchess Needy will do everything and anything to get and please a man. Unlike Lady Doormat, she gives everything and requires that he reciprocate. Not only is she afraid to lose him, her happiness depends on him. Therefore, she cannot be happy without him. She needs him in order to feel happy, whole, complete, and worthy. At her core, Duchess Needy feels unworthy and insecure. Her desire to be "close" to her man can be an ego stroke initially, but often has him quickly feeling smothered, overwhelmed, and tired. Soon he runs for the hills because he realizes that her needs are insatiable.

QUEEN I'M GOOD: Queen I'm Good can meet all her own needs. She shrouds herself in an air of independence. She has created a full and complete life all by herself, and "really, there is no space for anyone else." Queen I'm Good has wonderful BFFs, a great career, guys she can call for a quickie and/or a BOB, lots of hobbies and interests, and can fill her time in any way she chooses. If she meets someone, she ensures that he knows all of the above immediately. At the core, Queen I'm Good fears that she will never find a mate who can take care of her, so there is no room for hope. As a matter of fact, hope is hopeless and might even be a sign of weakness, she thinks. Queen I'm Good often comes off as either unavailable or uninterested in a relationship, which makes her unapproachable or a booty call—both of which reinforce her core belief. She can make her guy feel like a useless accessory.

MS. INTELLECTUAL: Ms. Intellectual presents as extraordinarily logical. She relies on facts, the tangible, and the provable. She is not to be confused with an educated or highly intelligent woman. Ms. Intellectual doesn't present this way because she's extremely smart. She presents this way because she doesn't want to allow her "feeling" self to be present. At the core, she is afraid of emotional vulnerability, so she "thinks" instead of "feels." Ms. Intellectual often confuses the guys she dates. He often doesn't feel connected to her because she shields her emotional self and presents like a robot. Her guy quickly tires of knocking and soon loses interest.

SHE FEELING: She Feeling is deeply emotional. She Feeling might cry at the drop of a hat, scream at level ten, and passionately kiss, all within minutes of each other or all in the same day or daily. The point is that her responses are often emotionally driven, reactive, and intense. Whether it's love, anger, or any feeling in between, She Feeling is ruled by them. At the core, She Feeling hasn't learned to regulate intense feelings and is easily flooded when faced with emotional triggers. In intimate relationships she feels and has difficulty thinking. Her man might initially be drawn to her intense passion, but that passion quickly turns to extreme sadness, anger, or even violence.

MILADY FEET FIRST: Milady Feet First is all-in from the very beginning. From the first date, she sees her possible husband, he's the one, and she is in love. Very soon after she meets him, she is looking at wedding venues, daydreaming about their romantic vacations, and naming their children. She tells her family, friends, and coworkers about him and immediately gives him total access to her life. Milady Feet First is more than happy to sleep with him on the first date, because they are soul mates, of course. Be careful not to confuse Milady Feet First with Duchess Needy. Milady Feet First doesn't necessarily need a man. At the core, often, she simply has poor boundaries and prefers the joy of fantasy to the pain of reality. To many men, Milady Feet First isn't seen as serious potential, because they don't have to work to get her.

PRINCESS MATERIAL GIRL: Princess Material Girl is all about what she has, what he has, and what she can get. Princess Material Girl judges others based on the visibility of their material possessions. She is interested in names, the four Cs (cut, carat, color, and clarity), little light-blue boxes, nice cars, and anything else that signifies status and money. Princess Material Girl is different from a gold digger in that she may have her own money and is not necessarily looking for a man to take care of her. She has a lifestyle that she enjoys, and she wants a man who "fits" into that lifestyle and shares her values as well. Princess Material Girl finds happiness in things and the attention that those things bring. At the core, Princess Material Girl likes status and recognition. She finds her worth in things and in others noticing her. Many men won't even try with Princess Material Girl, for obvious reasons. Most will experience her as "high maintenance"—and let's face it, girls, most men don't want to work that hard.

COUNTESS NEVER ALONE: Countess Never Alone hops from one relationship to another. She has never gone more than a couple of weeks without a man in some iteration of a relationship. She dreads being by herself and is most comfortable being in a relationship. She doesn't see herself as needy; Countess Never Alone often presents as confident because she is not overly reliant on any one relationship. She might be monogamous, but she makes and keeps connections with several men so that when and if one relationship ends, she has someone in the wings ready to move into position. At the core, Countess Never Alone is afraid of loneliness. She fears the possibility of not being intimately connected to another, which for her is being "alone." To Countess Never Alone, alone means that she is abandoned, emotionally empty, and unworthy. Her guy might not realize that she is never alone until he uncovers her little black book, and then he feels cheated.

🧩 **SISTER C. POTENTIAL:** Sister C. Potential dates "projects." She meets really nice guys who are under construction. Her guys are always in the process of preparing to do something great. They have big dreams, great ideas, and a master plan. All they need is for Sister C. Potential's love and support to actualize their latent abilities. Often her guys are nice enough, genuine, and fun to be around, but they lack the ability to see their plans through. Sister C. Potential soon goes from cheerleader to coach to CEO of her man's dreams. Underneath it all, Sister C. Potential often has a savior complex. At the core, she has an unconscious need to take care of someone and to have played a role in "making" someone or "saving" someone. Her behavior reinforces his underachievement, however, and causes her to become resentful. This dynamic further reinforces her need to do, because she does it all for him under a veil of help and support.

Did any of these ladies sound familiar? Did you see yourself in one or more of the descriptions? Trust me, this is not uncommon. Most of us don't neatly fit into just one; we might have a few behaviors from each lady. It is not the behaviors themselves that cause trouble in relationships. It is the intensity, the rigidity, and the consistency with which they are exhibited that can cause challenges.

Reflection: Let's Play the Dating Name Game

🦋 Reflect on your relationship traits. It might be helpful to think of yourself sitting in a movie theater watching a film. This can help you step outside of yourself and act as an observer. The film stars a woman who physically resembles you, and the story line follows her dating life, which is exactly like yours. As you watch, you begin to see patterns unfold and have some thoughts about what she's doing and how it is impacting the dynamics of the relationship.

🦋 Think of a cute name for the star of the film that captures the behaviors and traits of the character. Name of the leading lady:

_____

🦋 How would you describe her? (Refer to the examples on the preceding pages.) How does she behave? What are her traits? How does she attempt to get what she needs from her guy?

_____
_____
_____
_____
_____
_____
_____
_____
_____
_____
_____
_____
_____

🦋 When is _____ most likely to show up in all her glory?

_____

_____

_____

_____

_____

🦋 What effect(s) does _____ have on my life?

_____

_____

_____

_____

_____

🦋 What do I think about the effect(s) _____ is having on my dating life?

_____

_____

_____

_____

_____

_____

🦋 At her core, _____ is longing for

_____

_____

_____

_____

It is not necessary to change _____ , but acknowledge that holding on to her in the present form limits the pool of potential men who will be compatible with you. In the extreme, these behaviors can be difficult for your partner to cope with and might cause him to feel that the relationship is toxic. However, if we believe that there is someone for everyone, then we must believe that there is a man out there who will love your whiny, insecure, nagging, jealous behaviors all the way to the altar. Nevertheless, you might have to kiss a million more frogs to find that one who can and will tolerate _____.
Whether you decide to work on those traits or not, it is important for you to be aware of who you are in a relationship and how that might impact its success.

Reflection

🦋 Will I hold on to _____, make minor changes, or do a complete overhaul? Record your decision and reflect on why you made the choice you did and how you expect future dating to be impacted because of your decision.

_____

_____

_____

_____

_____

_____

_____

_____

_____

_____

_____

_____

_____

HOW DO OTHERS SEE ME?

In the previous section, you were asked to reflect on and identify behaviors that you notice in yourself. But we all have blind spots when it comes to ourselves. Many people spend thousands of dollars and multiple years trying to uncover aspects of themselves that they are unaware of. The way that we interact and relate to others seems "normal" and rational to us because it is the way that we learned people behave. Often we behave in a way that we believe conveys a universal message; however, this is far from the truth. How people perceive our behaviors can differ vastly. Our helpful behaviors can be interpreted as bossy. Our concern can be seen as intrusive. Our sweet nature can come across as weak. Let me be clear: I am in no way suggesting that you should be overly concerned with what people think about you. What I am talking about is actually the complete opposite. This relates more to what I discussed in the beginning of chapter 2. Are your behaviors congruent? Does your behavior accurately portray/relay your intent? Does the picture that you have of yourself actually match what people see?

 Identify at least two people (ideally three) you trust, who are pretty stable and who know you well. These folks can be male or female, family or friends, exes or besties. Talk to each one individually and let them know that you are in the process of preparing yourself to date with purpose and you need their opinion about you. Ask them to give you the "Describe Me as You See Me" assessment. Ask them to be honest, but they should not be cruel. They should tell you three positive things you do that contribute to a healthy relationship. They should have firsthand knowledge of these behaviors and traits in you. Then ask them to tell you about two areas of needed growth, from their perspective, that currently interfere with successful dating.

DESCRIBE ME AS YOU SEE ME

MY BEST ASSETS/POSITIVE TRAITS IN RELATIONSHIPS	AREAS OF NEEDED GROWTH IN RELATIONSHIPS
Name:	
1. 2. 3.	1. 2.
Name:	
1. 2. 3.	1. 2.
Name:	
1. 2. 3.	1. 2.

🦋 What feelings came up for me as I heard my friends talk about my positives? Do I notice these qualities in myself?

_____

_____

_____

_____

_____

_____

_____

_____

_____

_____

_____

🦋 What feelings came up for me as I heard my friends talk about my areas of needed growth? Do I notice these as areas that need growth?

_____

_____

_____

_____

_____

_____

_____

_____

_____

_____

_____

_____

Compare and contrast what you identified in your Dating Name Game to what your friends identified in you. What are the similarities? What are the differences? What surprised you?

_____

_____

_____

_____

_____

_____

_____

_____

_____

_____

_____

_____

_____

_____

_____

_____

_____

_____

_____

_____

_____

_____

_____

_____

_____

Reflect on who you have been in relationships. What was the impact of these traits on your past relationships? Take a moment to be honest with yourself. This exercise is not an opportunity to be overly critical or judgmental of yourself but rather a chance to become consciously aware of how you influence the ways that your relationships develop and ultimately end.

What was my role in co-creating the good, the bad, and the ugly dynamics of my last two to three relationships? In this reflection, don't spend any time writing about or rehashing what he did. Take some time to reflect on how your behavior shaped your relationship dance. Think of things like your overt and covert behaviors, your follow-through, your personality, character traits, et cetera.

🦋 My last relationship:

_____

_____

_____

_____

_____

_____

_____

_____

_____

_____

_____

_____

_____

_____

_____

_____

_____

_____

_____

_____

_____

_____

_____

✖ My second-to-last relationship:

_____
_____
_____
_____
_____
_____
_____
_____
_____
_____
_____
_____
_____

✖ The relationship before that one:

_____
_____
_____
_____
_____
_____
_____
_____
_____
_____
_____
_____

Reflection

🦋 What did I learn about my role in the co-creation of relationships?

_____

_____

_____

_____

_____

_____

_____

_____

_____

_____

🦋 What feelings came up for me as I think about my contribution to the demise of my relationships?

_____

_____

_____

_____

_____

_____

_____

_____

_____

_____

_____

🦋 What am I still struggling to accept as I think about my role in the failure of past relationships?

_____

_____

_____

_____

_____

_____

_____

_____

🦋 What would help me begin to accept that my behaviors co-created a dynamic that led to the breakups?

_____

_____

_____

_____

_____

_____

_____

_____

🦋 Now list three ways you can reduce the negative impact that your behavior will have on your next relationship.

_____

_____

_____

_____

_____

_____

_____

THE PAST, PRESENT, AND FUTURE

The most important thing a father can do for his children is to love their mother.

—Theodore Hesburgh

In addition to reflecting on the demise of your previous relationships, it is also important to reflect on what you learned from the relationships that you saw growing up. How did your primary caregivers—those you spent significant amounts of time with (mother, father, grandmother, grandfather, etc.)—"do" relationships? Often those relationships shape our ideas and fantasies about how relationships are formed, how we should behave in them, and what we can expect from our partner. Our parents are our first models for everything that we come to know about the world. Whether they are active in our lives or not, their presence or absence can teach us a lot. In essence, our parents are our blueprint for our understanding of life and the world. We learn this by watching how they relate to us and how they relate to others. This is especially true when it comes to intimate/love relationships. The relationship (or lack thereof) between our parents and caregivers shapes how we manage relationships and dating in adulthood. Of course, we are not destined to repeat the exact same triumphs or mistakes of our parents, nor are we fated to turn out exactly like them. But the examples we are given by our parents play a *huge* part in how we'll conduct our own love lives as adults. Hence, it is worth exploring what we might have picked up from them.

The early relationship that we have with our parents influences the views that we have of ourselves, others, and the world. In a nutshell, when we were younger, the way that our parents interacted with us told us something about ourselves (i.e., what we are "worthy" of), something about people/others (i.e., what we can expect from those outside of ourselves), and something about the larger world of which we are a part (i.e., what we can broadly expect from it). Similarly, we learned something about ourselves, others, and the world by observing how our parents interacted with others.

The chart below provides examples of various situations that children experience, how experiences might be internalized, and how they color perceptions.

EXPERIENCE	VIEW OF SELF	VIEW OF OTHERS	VIEW OF THE WORLD
Violence/abuse	I'm not safe.	People are dangerous.	The world is deadly.
Affair	I'm insignificant.	People are untrustworthy.	The world is undependable.
Distant	I'm alone.	People don't care.	The world is rejecting.
Divorce	I'm unloved/ unwanted.	People are unreliable.	The world is cruel.
Collaborative	I am good.	People are agreeable.	The world is cooperative.
Supportive	I am worthy.	People are caring.	The world is available.
Affectionate	I am lovable.	People are compassionate.	The world is kind.
Available	I am valuable.	People are well-intentioned.	The world is accessible.

There is a tendency to repeat these patterns if we do not make a conscious effort to do something different. Use the list of sample adjectives below to describe your parents' relationship while you were growing up. The list is not exhaustive. Feel free to use other adjectives that more appropriately match your memories. It is important to try very hard to have a balanced perspective. No person or relationship is perfect; conversely, no person or relationship is 100 percent horrible. Good and bad exist in everyone and in every relationship. Your task is to spend time thinking about both aspects of the relationships you witnessed.

ADJECTIVES			
Busy	Bored	Disloyal	Faithful
Happy	Hardworking	Intimidating	Communicative
Kind	Fussy	Miserable	Sensitive
Moody	Tense	Dangerous	Critical
Aggressive	Bossy	Hostile	Violent
Cranky	Rude	Malicious	Forgiving
Angry	Affectionate	Loving	Reliable
Considerate	Selfish	Compromising	Sincere
Worried	Caring	Committed	Thoughtful
Playful	Dishonest	Honest	Trustworthy
Gentle	Stingy	Available	Close
Disrespectful	Loyal	Flaky	Dysfunctional
Argumentative	Absent	Manipulative	_____
Selfless	_____	_____	_____
_____	_____	_____	_____
_____	_____	_____	_____
_____	_____	_____	_____

🦋 (If your parents/caregivers <u>were</u> married or together for the majority of your childhood) Name at least eight adjectives to describe your parents' relationship with each other.

_____

_____

_____

_____

_____

_____

🦋 (If your parents/caregivers <u>weren't</u> married or together for the majority of your childhood) Name at least eight adjectives to describe your <u>mother's/caregiver's</u> intimate relationships.

_____

_____

_____

🦋 (If your parents/caregivers <u>weren't</u> married or together for the majority of your childhood) Name at least eight adjectives to describe your <u>father's/caregiver's</u> intimate relationships.

_____

_____

_____

🦋 Circle the five most powerful descriptions of your parents or caregivers above, and write them in the Experience column. Then spend some time thinking about how the experience of witnessing these behaviors while growing up has shaped your views of yourself, others, and the world.

EXPERIENCE	VIEW OF SELF	VIEW OF OTHERS	VIEW OF THE WORLD

Reflect on your answers above. How did the relationships that you saw while growing up influence your current relationship patterns? Are there any similarities?

_____

_____

_____

_____

_____

_____

_____

_____

_____

_____

_____

_____

_____

_____

_____

_____

_____

_____

_____

_____

_____

_____

_____

_____

_____

How do your views of yourself and others impact how you date and how you are in relationships? What do you expect, and what are you willing to give?

_____

_____

_____

_____

_____

_____

_____

_____

_____

_____

_____

_____

_____

_____

_____

_____

_____

_____

_____

_____

_____

_____

_____

_____

_____

_____

_____

_____

_____

Think about what was missing in your childhood. This exercise is not designed to bash the adults who were in your life or to dismiss all the wonderful things that they've done. No one is perfect; nor is anyone all good or all bad. Nor can anyone be all things to you or provide everything you need at all times. These exercises provide you with an opportunity to acknowledge that 100 percent of your needs could not be met 100 percent of the time.

For this next exercise, think about the relationships that you had with two primary adults in your life. This can be your parents or primary caregivers. In the first column, list the positive qualities about those relationships.

For example, were they *open, welcoming, affectionate, trustworthy, loving, warm, fun, funny, supportive, encouraging, available?* Did you feel *valuable, wanted, beautiful, smart, included, safe, accepted, et cetera?*

In the second column, describe negative qualities, things that were missing from the relationships/interactions, and things that you desired but didn't receive. Remember, there are no right or wrong answers here, only honest answers.

PARENT/CAREGIVER #1

POSITIVE RELATIONSHIP QUALITIES	NEGATIVE, MISSING, OR DESIRED

PARENT/CAREGIVER #2

POSITIVE RELATIONSHIP QUALITIES	NEGATIVE, MISSING, OR DESIRED

🦋 How have your positive experiences in early childhood relationships impacted your dating and intimate relationships now? How and when do they show up?

_____

_____

_____

_____

_____

_____

_____

_____

_____

_____

_____

🦋 How have your negative experiences and the things that you missed in your early childhood relationships impacted your dating and intimate relationships now? How and when do they show up?

_____

_____

_____

_____

_____

_____

_____

_____

_____

_____

_____

How do the childhood experiences discussed above relate to your answers in the Dating Name Game? Describe any connections between the qualities exhibited by the star of the "movie" and your experiences.

_____

_____

_____

_____

_____

_____

_____

_____

_____

_____

_____

_____

_____

_____

_____

_____

_____

_____

_____

_____

_____

_____

_____

_____

_____

How to Keep the Past from Dictating Your Future

⊞ Acknowledge what happened.

A pervasive running joke about psychology is that "everything is your mother's fault." Statements like this are problematic for several reasons. They are used sarcastically to discredit and over-simplify psychological theory. Additionally, they minimize the importance of understanding how childhood experiences impact adult behavior. They can send people into protective mode, where they refuse to acknowledge any unhappy childhood experiences in the home, thus refusing to acknowledge that they learned some unhealthy things about relationships from the ones who potentially love them the most. However, we cannot change what we do not own. Acknowledging is not blaming. It is not saying that your caregivers were mean, horrible, evil people who ruined you. Acknowledging, in this context, is simply admitting that those who raised us were not perfect, and therefore we are not perfect. It is these imperfections that show up, in unhealthy ways, in our relationships.

⊞ Acknowledge the impact.

When we accept that we've had certain experiences, we must also acknowledge that our experiences have an impact on us (in some way). Our early experiences are internalized and color our relationship behavior. Many women will say things like "I don't want to be anything like my parent(s)" or "I want to have a relationship just like my parents'." Truthfully, neither of these statements is possible, because they are all-or-nothing, black-and-white statements. You cannot be "nothing" like your parent(s) or have a relationship that is "just" like your parents'. That is because you have different childhood experiences from each of your parents, and those experiences have impacted you in unique ways. Therefore, the way that you move on will be influenced by your parents but expressed in ways that only you can. Hopefully, the exercises in this chapter have helped to identify the ways that your childhood shows up in your relationships. If we don't acknowledge that we have been impacted, even if we vowed that we wouldn't be, we won't be able to actively recognize it when it is happening and choose to act differently.

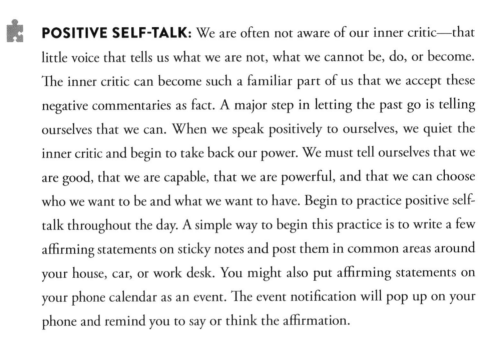

Choose to let it go.

In order to move on, you must not hold on to those ways that you were failed as a child. You must make a conscious effort to let go of your past hurts and engage in activities that help you to be the person you would like to be. Here are three things that can help you let go.

POSITIVE SELF-TALK: We are often not aware of our inner critic—that little voice that tells us what we are not, what we cannot be, do, or become. The inner critic can become such a familiar part of us that we accept these negative commentaries as fact. A major step in letting the past go is telling ourselves that we can. When we speak positively to ourselves, we quiet the inner critic and begin to take back our power. We must tell ourselves that we are good, that we are capable, that we are powerful, and that we can choose who we want to be and what we want to have. Begin to practice positive self-talk throughout the day. A simple way to begin this practice is to write a few affirming statements on sticky notes and post them in common areas around your house, car, or work desk. You might also put affirming statements on your phone calendar as an event. The event notification will pop up on your phone and remind you to say or think the affirmation.

PRACTICE SIMPLE MINDFULNESS: Simply put, practice staying in the moment. Rather than dwelling on the past or worrying about the future, focus on the now. Pay attention to the sights, sounds, and smells of now. Be aware of what is happening in your body and what you are feeling emotionally. Commit to living in the present and to being mindful of when sensations, thoughts, and feelings from the past begin to intrude on the present.

FORGIVE THEM: The act of forgiveness is very powerful and can be very difficult to do. Although some women completing chapter 2 might have found it difficult to identify unhealthy behaviors in their caregivers, others had no difficulty with this at all. Considering themselves survivors of chaotic, dysfunctional, and even abusive households, they suffered at the hand of "loved" ones. In either case, forgiveness equals freedom. When we don't forgive, we are psychologically and emotionally tied to the past. We live with the thoughts of what they did to us or what they did not do for us. The problem with this is that the past cannot be changed. It happened, it was painful, and now as an adult you do not have to tolerate it. These facts should help you to begin the process of forgiveness. Forgiveness is not saying that what was done was OK; it is about you releasing yourself from what you cannot change. Begin the process of forgiveness today.

Chapter 2 Reflection

🦋 What did I learn about myself in this chapter?

_____

_____

_____

_____

_____

_____

_____

_____

_____

_____

🦋 What did I learn about the impact my history has on my dating habits in this chapter?

_____

_____

_____

_____

_____

_____

_____

_____

_____

_____

🦋 How will I keep my past from negatively influencing my present?

_____

_____

_____

_____

_____

_____

_____

_____

_____

_____

🦋 What skills and tools did I learn in this chapter?

_____

_____

_____

_____

_____

_____

_____

_____

_____

_____

_____

3

Dating After Trauma

Instead of saying "I'm damaged, I'm broken, I have trust issues,"
say "I'm healing, I'm rediscovering myself, I'm starting over."

—*Horacio Jones*

TRAUMA

Some of you will see this chapter and wonder why it is included in a book about dating. Others of you will see this chapter and know exactly why it is included. Given what I have researched, read, studied, witnessed, and treated, I felt that I would miss an important dating factor if I didn't discuss trauma.

Current literature states that 91 percent of the victims of rape and sexual assault are female, and 81 percent of women report significant short-term or long-term impacts such as post-traumatic stress disorder. Given these statistics, it stands to reason that many women completing this workbook have a history of personal violation. I must emphasize that experiencing abuse and/or sexual violation doesn't automatically lead to problems with relationships in adulthood. However, the effects that such experiences have on many survivors can be long-lasting and insidious and can live outside of conscious awareness/understanding: the resulting symptoms can become such an integrated part of one's being that it is impossible to identify which came first. I have heard many women say, "I don't know. This is the way that I've always been" or "I just don't trust people—that's just how I am." This chapter is designed to increase awareness about the multifaceted psychological impact of trauma and the subtle ways that it can show up in your dating life.

Note: This chapter will discuss various aspects of trauma and has the potential to cause emotional discomfort for some survivors. If you know that you become emotionally, psychologically, or physically distressed when thinking about or discussing your past, please work through this chapter with a trained mental health provider in your area.

WHAT IS TRAUMA?

For a long time, the belief was that only people who fought in war experienced trauma. However, now the word is often used in everyday language to describe an event that was difficult, unpleasant, and caused stress and/or distress. Some people will say things like "we drove all the way to the concert and it was canceled; that was so traumatizing." The fact that the word trauma has moved from only being applicable to a certain part of the population to being used in casual conversation is both a blessing and a curse. The increased use of the word helps to destigmatize it and normalizes the aftereffects for survivors. However, broad use of the word can dilute its significance and minimize the significance of the horrific events experienced by survivors. In essence, the word can become so commonplace that everything becomes trauma—and, therefore, nothing is trauma. For this reason, I think it is important to define what I mean by trauma in relation to dating.

The word *trauma* means *wound* in Greek. There are many different events that can cause overwhelming distress or a psychological wound. Some that are consistently recognized by experts in the field are: (a) experiencing, witnessing, or hearing about actual or threatened death; (b) actual or threatened serious bodily injury; and (c) actual or threatened sexual violence.

 Take time to reflect: Have you experienced trauma? Put a check mark next to any event that you have experienced personally, that you witnessed, or that you heard about happening to a family member or close friend.

SELF	SAW	OTHER	
			Physical assault
			Robbed
			Serious accident (work, home, leisure activities)
			Attempted murder
			Sexual assault (as adult)
			Military war deployment
			Kidnapped
			Been shot
			Industrial/traumatic injury
			Witnessed a murder
			Taken from primary caregivers
			Car crash
			Plane crash
			Physical abuse (as adult)
			Bullying
			Home invasion
			Physical abuse (as child)
			Natural disaster
			Witnessed someone else being shot
			Traumatic incarceration experiences
			Sexual assault (as child)
			Loss of parent(s) during childhood

What feelings come up for you as you review your responses to the checklist? Note any thoughts, feelings, bodily sensations.

_____

_____

_____

_____

_____

_____

_____

_____

_____

_____

_____

_____

_____

_____

_____

_____

_____

_____

_____

_____

_____

_____

_____

_____

_____

Many people are surprised by the number of traumatic events that they have experienced over their lifetime. It is not uncommon to think about each incident as an isolated event, without stopping to think of the sum of the various events. It is also not uncommon for memories or reminders of these events to trigger upsetting and difficult thoughts and feelings. But whether an event—as well as which event(s)—will continue to have an impact on you over your lifetime is dependent on a number of things.

THE IMPACT OF TRAUMA

The hallmarks of lasting psychological trauma stem from overwhelming events that are unexpected and outside of the normal realm of human experience and that overpower the usual methods of coping that give people a sense of control, connection, and meaning. We tend to think about trauma in a few different ways:

Personal/Secluded Events and Public/Shared Events

Traumatic events take many forms and occur in various settings. Personal/secluded events are those that often occur to one person (or a few, such as in a family) and have a degree of privacy. Public/shared traumatic events are major events that occur on a broader scale, affecting large numbers of people.

- **Examples of personal/secluded events:** sexual assault, sexual abuse, domestic violence, interpersonal violence, witnessing domestic violence.

- **Examples of public/shared events:** war, acts of terrorism, mass shootings, natural disasters, community violence.

Although each of these events on its own can cause lasting psychological symptoms that impact functioning, personal/secluded traumas have been found to be more troublesome for intimate relationships than the experience of natural disasters. This is because personal/secluded traumas occur at the hands of another person. They not only occur in the context of human interaction but most often in the context of relationships. When this happens, it challenges our basic sense of trust developed early in life. These events erode our belief in humanity and shatter any confidence that we can keep ourselves safe. Private traumatic events are also often followed by self-blame and guilt. Survivors often blame themselves and develop feelings of shame for not protecting themselves, or a belief that if they had done something different, the event could have been prevented. Sadly, these beliefs are often reinforced by society and others in the survivor's life. How many times have we heard sexual assault survivors being questioned about what they were wearing or why they were at a certain location? Even children are often asked why they didn't tell. These types of responses from others leave the survivor with a sense of responsibility for their violation.

🦋 Look back at the trauma checklist. Have you experienced any personal/secluded traumas? What were the responses of others when learning of your experience? How did their responses leave you feeling?

_____

_____

_____

_____

_____

_____

_____

_____

_____

_____

_____

_____

_____

_____

_____

_____

_____

_____

_____

_____

_____

_____

_____

_____

_____

_____

_____

_____

_____

_____

_____

_____

_____

_____

_____

_____

_____

_____

_____

_____

There are many feelings that can come up as a result of the responses from others. These internal reactions generally surface days, weeks, and even months after disclosure of the event. However, there are instantaneous feelings and reactions that occur during the incident and immediately after. These responses are the body's natural and voluntary reactions to a terrible event.

Below are common feelings and reactions following trauma. Put a check mark next to any feelings that you remember having after your trauma.

COMMON FEELINGS AND REACTIONS FOLLOWING A TRAUMA

❏ Shock, denial, or disbelief

❏ Confusion

❏ Anger, irritability, mood swings

❏ Anxiety and fear

❏ Guilt, shame, self-blame

❏ Withdrawing from others

❏ Feeling sad or hopeless

❏ Feeling disconnected or numb

❏ Feeling hopeless about the future

❏ Feeling detached or unconcerned about others

❏ Having trouble making decisions

❏ Feeling jumpy

❏ Feeling on guard and constantly alert

❏ Having disturbing dreams and memories or flashbacks

❏ The development of work or school problems

❏ Insomnia or nightmares

❏ Fatigue

❏ Being startled easily

❏ Difficulty concentrating

❏ Racing heartbeat

❏ Edginess and agitation

❏ Aches and pains

❏ Muscle tension

Longer-term effects may include emotional troubles such as:

❏ Feeling nervous, helpless, fearful, sad

❏ Feeling shocked, numb, and not able to feel love or joy

❏ Avoiding people, places, and things related to the event

❏ Becoming easily upset or agitated

❏ Blaming yourself or having negative views of oneself or the world

❏ Distrust of others, getting into conflicts, being overcontrolling

❏ Being withdrawn, feeling rejected or abandoned

❏ Loss of intimacy or feeling detached

What feelings come up for you as you review your responses to the checklist? Note any thoughts, feelings, bodily sensations.

_____

_____

_____

_____

_____

_____

_____

_____

_____

_____

_____

_____

_____

_____

_____

_____

_____

_____

_____

_____

_____

_____

_____

_____

_____

_____

_____

Most people will experience trauma-related symptoms following exposure to trauma or a series of traumas. But many people will begin to feel better with the support of family and friends. Put a check mark next to any feelings that you have had in the past twelve months.

COMMON FEELINGS AND REACTIONS FOLLOWING A TRAUMA

❏ Shock, denial, or disbelief
❏ Confusion
❏ Anger, irritability, mood swings
❏ Anxiety and fear
❏ Guilt, shame, self-blame
❏ Withdrawing from others
❏ Feeling sad or hopeless
❏ Feeling disconnected or numb
❏ Feeling hopeless about the future
❏ Feeling detached or unconcerned about others
❏ Having trouble making decisions
❏ Feeling jumpy
❏ Feeling on guard and constantly alert
❏ Having disturbing dreams and memories or flashbacks
❏ The development of work or school problems
❏ Insomnia or nightmares
❏ Fatigue
❏ Being startled easily
❏ Difficulty concentrating

❏ Racing heartbeat
❏ Edginess and agitation
❏ Aches and pains
❏ Muscle tension

Longer-term effects may include emotional troubles such as:

❏ Feeling nervous, helpless, fearful, sad
❏ Feeling shocked, numb, and not able to feel love or joy
❏ Avoiding people, places, and things related to the event
❏ Becoming easily upset or agitated
❏ Blaming yourself or having negative views of oneself or the world
❏ Distrust of others, getting into conflicts, being overcontrolling
❏ Being withdrawn, feeling rejected or abandoned
❏ Loss of intimacy or feeling detached

What feelings come up for you as you review your responses to the checklist? Note any thoughts, feelings, bodily sensations.

_____

_____

_____

_____

_____

_____

_____

_____

_____

_____

_____

_____

_____

_____

_____

_____

_____

_____

_____

_____

_____

_____

_____

_____

_____

_____

TRAUMA AND RELATIONSHIPS

It is true that not all women who have experienced private or personal traumas will develop difficulty in intimate relationships. However, any and all residual symptoms can have a huge impact. If it is challenging for you to understand or manage your symptoms, imagine how your potential partner might feel. For many, it is easier to identify and deal with the more physical and emotional symptoms, because they are often within our awareness. We (and those around us) are often able to label our feelings and notice physical changes. However, changes in our sense of self may be less immediately noticeable but can have a direct and immediate effect on developing a new relationship or maintaining the relationship that you have. Changes related to broken trust, impaired boundaries, personal beliefs, emotional reactions, and intimacy difficulties can go unnoticed for months or even years. The changes in and of themselves are not necessarily the issue. It is when those changes become rigidly polarized that they can become very troublesome to you and your date.

TRUST

Trust is one of the most important aspects of a healthy relationship. Sexual violation at any age can affect a woman's ability to trust others and herself. When the abuse is perpetrated by someone that she loves and trusts, which is often the case in childhood, she might have feelings both of love and pain. This causes an internal conflict. She is confused by loving someone who is causing her pain. She can begin to distrust her own feelings and/or sense that her feelings have betrayed her. As discussed in chapter 2, these early relationships become a blueprint for love. Therefore, pain and betrayal are seen as a normal part of love. Likewise, given the interpersonal nature of physical and sexual abuse, whether the abuse occurred as a child or an adult, people become untrustworthy. Without actively addressing these experiences, she will walk into relationships not trusting herself, not trusting her man, or both. On one extreme, she might become so closed off that she won't let anyone emotionally close as a way of protecting against painful betrayal from untrustworthy people. On the other end of the continuum, she might blindly walk into abusive, unhealthy relationships because they feel familiar, predictable, and safe.

WAYS TRAUMA MAY IMPACT TRUST

TOO TRUSTING	NOT TRUSTING
• You believe what people say even when there is evidence to the contrary.	• You are suspicious of what most people tell you most of the time.
• You discuss your personal business very quickly.	• You are guarded and feel the need to protect yourself from the motives of others.
• You rarely ask or observe for tangible confirmation of what he says.	• People have told you that you are difficult to get to know.
• Once the relationship has ended, you often feel taken advantage of.	• You generally believe that most people lie.
• You give him access to your finances after a few dates.	• People need to prove that they can be trusted.
• Family and friends have told you that you are too trusting.	• Once the relationship has ended, you often feel "I knew it."

BOUNDARIES

There is an in-depth discussion of boundaries in chapter 5. Here, it is important to understand that experiences of abuse can have a significant impact on the survivor's ability to establish healthy boundaries in relationships. All abuse, whether physical or sexual, is an invasion of the survivor's boundaries. During the event(s), the victim experiences a complete loss of control over their lives and their bodies. Survivors, especially those abused in childhood, never have an opportunity to learn that they have the right to control what happens to them and what doesn't. Those violated in adulthood might begin to believe that boundaries are useless because they are unable to protect themselves anyway. Or they might develop overly strict boundaries, seeing any flexibility as dangerous.

BELIEFS

Abuse and violations can impact the survivor's beliefs about themselves and others. This is largely related to the way that the survivor internalizes the cause and ascribes meaning to the event. As mentioned earlier, given the traditional societal response, it is easy for the survivors to blame themselves for the event and to second-guess their actions before, during, and after the event. These self-deprecating thoughts can relate to acts that occur in childhood or adulthood. Survivors can question whether they did something to cause the perpetrator's anger in the case of physical abuse or whether they enticed the perpetrator in the case of sexual abuse. In either case, the survivor's beliefs can morph into self-blame and shame. In the case of sexual abuse, survivors can interpret automatic physical responses as pleasure and begin to believe that they enjoyed it; therefore, a belief of responsibility may develop. Additionally, the survivor might develop beliefs about the perpetrator that are in direct contrast to the beliefs about themselves. They might begin to see the perpetrator as powerful, in control, inescapable, and invincible They might also begin to have sympathy for their abuser as a result of believing that they have some fault in the abuse or violation.

 Take a moment to reflect on the beliefs that you have about yourself and your beliefs about what you can expect from others.

EXPERIENCE	VIEW OF SELF	VIEW OF OTHERS	VIEW OF THE WORLD

How might your experience of trauma impact your beliefs?

_____

_____

_____

_____

_____

_____

_____

_____

_____

_____

_____

_____

_____

_____

_____

_____

_____

_____

_____

_____

_____

_____

_____

_____

_____

█ EMOTIONS

The experience of physical abuse, sexual abuse, or assault is extremely emotionally overwhelming and distressing. As a result, many survivors develop difficulty regulating their emotions. Brain research has shown that abuse in childhood can result in an altered biological response to very stressful situations. Similarly, adult survivors can develop an impaired ability to tolerate stress and negative emotional states. This can cause them to have amplified reactions to common relationship problems. These reactions can be exhibited as extremely aggressive, taking the form of emotionally fueled disputes, anger, crying, and/or outbursts, or as extremely passive, taking the form of emotional withdrawal, isolation/unresponsive behavior, or fleeing. They might find it difficult to accept love, and the very act of affection might evoke an emotional threat response.

The technical term for this is emotional dysregulation. Emotional dysregulation occurs when your emotional reaction is out of proportion given the situation or when your emotional reaction doesn't fit the facts at all. You might also have difficulty soothing yourself when you're upset or bothered by something, and you experience embarrassment, confusion, and bewilderment about your emotions. Emotional dysregulation is almost always triggered in the context of close interpersonal relationships.

The following checklist is not meant to diagnose but rather to increase your awareness of how your emotions might be showing up.

- ❏ I experience my emotions very strongly.
- ❏ I am unable to verbalize my emotions often.
- ❏ I experience my emotions as overwhelming and out of control.
- ❏ When I'm upset I am 100 percent sure that my feelings are valid.
- ❏ I am often confused about how I feel.
- ❏ When upset, I often become out of control.
- ❏ When I become upset, I feel out of control.
- ❏ When upset, I have difficulty remaining in control of my behaviors.
- ❏ It can take me a long time to feel better once I become upset.
- ❏ I have been told by several people that I often overreact to situations.

The fact is, each of these can have an impact on intimacy. If you checked any one of these, you might want to talk to a professional for a more-formal assessment. If you checked three or more of these, you should seriously consider working with a professional to gain tools to help you to better handle strong emotions. When recovering from a person-to-person violation, you are forced to learn new ways to cope with the experience. You must learn a new way of being in order to move forward with your life. You learn to cope with people's untrustworthiness, the shattered sense of safety, the beliefs that you have about yourself and others, and feelings of intense emotions. Regardless of the guy that you meet, these old ways of coping will still be in play. They were developed to keep you safe, to give meaning to your experience and your life afterward, and they helped you to survive. Now you must begin to learn new survival techniques that help you establish healthy connections with others.

Chapter 3 Reflection

🦋 What did I learn about myself in this chapter?

_____

_____

_____

_____

_____

_____

_____

_____

_____

_____

_____

🦋 What did I learn in this chapter about the impact my trauma history has on my dating habits?

_____

_____

_____

_____

_____

_____

_____

_____

_____

_____

_____

_____

🦋 What do I need to do to keep my trauma history from negatively impacting my present?

_____

_____

_____

_____

_____

_____

_____

_____

_____

_____

_____

_____

_____

4

I Know Him

Then I realize what it is. It's him. Something about him makes me feel
like I am about to fall. Or turn to liquid. Or burst into flames.

—Veronica Roth

Who is this guy? Who are you attracted to? What about "him" lights your fire? What about that fire continues to burn? Have you ever thought about it? We are not taught to look at patterns between the men that we date. Because we don't look, we don't often see the commonalities in them. As a matter of fact, we tend to make a verbal commitment not to repeat the same mistake ("I'll never date a guy who is mean to his mother again"). When we focus on his overt observable bad behaviors, we might get a guy who is not mean to his mother but is mean to everyone else, including you. By looking at specific behaviors and not connecting patterns, we end up getting the same present wrapped in different paper. Most of us are "drawn" to a type. For some it might be looks, for others it might be swagger, and there are those who are drawn to his unavailability. Whatever it is, I can guarantee that you are drawn to him (any him) because something about him is familiar. This familiarity is often not conscious or something that you can articulate. It is more of a feeling, an inner connection to a part of you with a longing. Understanding that part is essential to dating with purpose.

THE WOMAN IN THE MIRROR

If you're searching for that one person who will change your life, look within.

—Unknown

In the same way that our ideas about who we are and how to have relationships are shaped by our early experiences, so are our unconscious prototypes of an ideal mate. As we are growing up, we learn how to give love and how to receive love, what to expect when in love, and the "meaning" of love. We learn what to expect, how to expect it, when to expect it, and from whom to expect it. This shapes our emotional love blueprint. In adulthood, many develop a logical understanding of what healthy love looks and feels like. However, many often still find themselves in relationships that are painful, unfulfilling, and unhealthy. There are several reasons for this scenario. We are emotionally attracted to what feels familiar. And . . .

- Although we might say that we want a guy who will love and cherish us, we are attracted to the guy who has limited capacity to do so because it reminds us of a familiar pain of childhood (in some ways the abnormal has become normal).

- We have poor boundaries (no dealbreakers).

- We believe that a piece is good enough (fear of being alone).

- We love fixer-uppers (caretaker).

- We don't think we deserve any better (low self-esteem).

- They are a mirror (we see ourselves in them).

Whether it is one of the above or one that I did not mention, there was something in each guy from the past that complemented a piece of you.

You will notice that this chapter is relatively short. Although looking in the rearview mirror provides crucial information, our focus must be on the windshield if we are to get to where we are going. It is important for us to reflect on what we have done in the past only long enough to learn what not to do in the future. Additionally, the goal is not for you to dwell on him but to look at what in you was attracted to all that he was. This chapter will give you an opportunity to think about a few of the men from your past and what part of you was tantalized by his being.

I LIKE THAT

Life can only be understood backwards; but it must be lived forward.

—*Søren Kierkegaard*

How many times have you sat back after a relationship ended and said to yourself, "What was I doing?" It was not until he was gone that you admitted to yourself that you knew it was never going to work. Maybe this thought bubbled up early on, like when you first met, or maybe it came up after you had been dating for a while. In either case, you used hope to mute that little eternal voice and gave it a chance. On the other hand, you could be one who continues to question, "What happened?" You are still baffled by the breakup because from your vantage point "things were going so well." You never saw the red flags, or you might even say "there were no red flags to see." Yet again, you may be one who listened to that voice, saw the signs, and ran for the hills, repeatedly. Regardless of the scenario, there was something in him that you wanted, and that something interfered with your vision and decisions. Yes, even if you are leaving "unhealthy" relationships, reflecting on what you are attracting can give you insight about what you are projecting.

As you complete the exercises in this chapter, be fair and honest with yourself. Try not to let your feelings for the fellow influence your ability to give an honest and balanced picture of what you saw in him and who he was. He couldn't have been all bad or you wouldn't have had the good times that you did with him (even if they were few and far between). Likewise, he couldn't have been your perfect match or you wouldn't have said goodbye (if you thought he was perfect and he didn't reciprocate, that was a sign that he wasn't perfect).

In the following exercise, reflect on two or three guys from your past. Don't rush through this exercise. It might take you a couple of days to think about answers for each question. Allow yourself to come back to the questions periodically as you recall information. If you kept a journal while dating, reading what you wrote during the time might help you recall what you thought and felt in the moment.

Time to Think About Him

 What traits attracted me to him?

1. NAME

THINGS/TRAITS I LIKED	THINGS/TRAITS I DISLIKED

 What attracted me most to him:

_____

_____

_____

_____

🦋 The good/healthy things about the relationship were:

_____

_____

_____

_____

_____

_____

_____

_____

_____

_____

_____

_____

🦋 The bad/unhealthy things were:

_____

_____

_____

_____

_____

_____

_____

_____

_____

_____

_____

_____

🦋 I first began to question whether to leave after _____ *(how long into the relationship?)*. Describe the situation that made you consider leaving for the first time:

_____
_____
_____
_____
_____
_____
_____

🦋 I stayed with him _____ years _____ months. I stayed that long because:

_____
_____
_____
_____
_____
_____
_____
_____

🦋 What did I learn about myself as a result of reflecting on this relationship? What in him complemented what in me?

_____
_____
_____
_____
_____
_____
_____

2. NAME

THINGS/TRAITS I LIKED	THINGS/TRAITS I DISLIKED

🦋 What attracted me most to him:

_____

_____

_____

_____

🦋 The good/healthy things about the relationship were:

_____

_____

_____

_____

_____

🦋 The bad/unhealthy things were:

_____

_____

_____

_____

_____

🦋 I first began to question whether to leave after _____ *(how long into the relationship?)*. Describe the situation that made you consider leaving for the first time:

_____
_____
_____
_____
_____
_____
_____

🦋 I stayed with him _____ years _____ months. I stayed that long because:

_____
_____
_____
_____
_____
_____
_____
_____

🦋 What did I learn about myself as a result of reflecting on this relationship? What in him complemented what in me?

_____
_____
_____
_____
_____
_____
_____

3. NAME

THINGS/TRAITS I LIKED	THINGS/TRAITS I DISLIKED

🦋 What attracted me most to him:

_____

_____

_____

_____

_____

🦋 The good/healthy things about the relationship were:

_____

_____

_____

_____

_____

🦋 The bad/unhealthy things were:

_____

_____

_____

_____

_____

🦋 I first began to question whether to leave after _____ *(how long into the relationship?)*. Describe the situation that made you consider leaving for the first time:

_____

_____

_____

_____

_____

_____

_____

🦋 I stayed with him _____ years _____ months. I stayed that long because:

_____

_____

_____

_____

_____

_____

_____

🦋 What did I learn about myself as a result of reflecting on this relationship? What in him complemented what in me?

_____

_____

_____

_____

_____

_____

_____

🦋 Look at each of your responses about the men that you have dated in the past. Circle repeated traits listed for each guy. Are there any overlaps in traits that you liked? List repeated traits.

_____

_____

_____

_____

_____

_____

_____

Find the patterns and complete these sentence stems, creating one long sentence for each that encompasses at least two positive and two negative traits. For example: In the past I have been attracted to really cute guys who drove nice cars, but they also didn't pursue me and were still not settled.

🦋 In the past I have been attracted to men who:

_____

_____

_____

_____

_____

🦋 I often dated men who (include at least two positive traits and two negative traits from above; be sure to include any that occur more than once):

_____

_____

_____

_____

_____

🦋 I often stayed longer than I should have because:

_____

_____

_____

_____

_____

🦋 Review your answers for each of the exercises in chapter 2. How did what you
discovered about yourself impact why you stayed?

_____

_____

_____

_____

_____

_____

_____

_____

_____

_____

_____

_____

_____

_____

_____

_____

_____

_____

Chapter 4 Reflection

🦋 What did I learn in this chapter about the men I'm attracted to?

_____

_____

_____

_____

_____

_____

_____

_____

_____

🦋 What did I learn in this chapter about my dating habits?

_____

_____

_____

_____

_____

_____

_____

_____

_____

_____

_____

🦋 What do I want to change about how I get into and how I get out of relationships in the future?

_____

_____

_____

_____

_____

_____

_____

_____

_____

_____

_____

🦋 What am I committed to doing to ensure that I don't repeat this pattern?

_____

_____

_____

_____

_____

_____

_____

_____

_____

_____

_____

_____

5

Date with Purpose

All our dreams can come true if we have the courage to pursue them.

—*Walt Disney*

Efforts and courage are not enough without purpose and direction.

—*John F. Kennedy*

Dating with purpose is not only a state of mind; it is also a skill. By completing this workbook to this point, you have already begun the process of understanding yourself in new ways. You have been introduced to the idea that dating with purpose is very different than dating out of desperation. You have made a commitment to complete exercises that require you to reflect on your personality traits, family history, past dating habits, et cetera, in an effort to become consciously aware of how you are co-creating relationships. In addition to this increased awareness, there must also be a focus on skills, increasing the "how to" of dating with purpose.

Remember that dating with purpose includes balancing your thinking brain with your emotional brain. The task is to ensure that your emotional brain doesn't hijack your thinking brain and vice versa. Therefore, in order to date with purpose, we first need to have a cognitive understanding of what we want and a strategy on how to get there. The remainder of this book focuses on building skills and providing tools to assist in developing more-effective dating behaviors.

FANTASYLAND

What is your fantasy of the ideal guy? Is he a tall hunk of a man who is independently wealthy, has an IQ above 120, and an emotional intelligence that makes others marvel? Does he love his mother, want a family, and lives to treat you like a queen? How do you dream of meeting him? Will your eyes lock across a crowded room? Will he bump into you (literally) at the neighborhood coffee shop and break the tension with his irresistible wit? Or will he be the keynote speaker at your work conference who will be introduced to you by your boss?

From the time we are born, little girls are socialized to fantasize about love. Classic fairy tales have the damsel in distress being saved by the knight in shining armor. One would think that in this millennium such a narrative would be unpopular, but quite the contrary. They live on and continue to be told as bedtime stories to little girls all around the world. In subtle ways (i.e., even the phrase "treated like a queen" implies having a king), women are told that he will be everything good, give us everything we desire, and make us feel like sunshine.

 Here is your chance to spend time in Fantasyland. Write down your fantasy man, the fantasy relationship you two will have, the life he will provide, fill, or help you to create, et cetera. Include as much detail as possible: looks, education, income, how you meet, what he says, what attracts you, what makes you swoon, and so on. This should be your "perfect" fantasy.

🦋 Read over your fantasy above. What feelings come up for you as you read it? Are there feelings of hope, anticipation, joy, or feelings of despair, hopelessness, sadness, or a combination?

_____

_____

_____

_____

_____

_____

_____

_____

_____

_____

_____

_____

_____

_____

_____

_____

_____

_____

_____

_____

As you might imagine, there are both pros and cons to fantasizing about "him." Let's look at five cons.

Potential Problems with Fantasizing

SIMPLE: Fantasies are often overly simplistic and rarely encompass the complexities of life. Fantasies generally proceed in a very straightforward and linear fashion. They unfold in an orderly fashion, from point A to B. Most do not include navigating complicated work schedules, family dynamics, distance, et cetera. These realities are not necessarily negative, but they are inevitable. Those who rely heavily on fantasies can be overwhelmed when obstacles present themselves. Some may even interpret them as a sign that he is not Mr. Right.

POSITIVE: Most fantasies about him are often overly positive. Generally, he is the most handsome, the most affectionate, the most loving, and the list goes on. Rarely do we fantasize about negative character traits, beliefs, or behaviors that he might possess. Given that a perfect person does not exist, you can bet your purposeful behind that he will show up with something that will get on your nerves. He might snore, chew with his mouth open, be allergic to your long-haired cat, have bad credit, et cetera.

DECREASES EFFORT: Some of the research on fantasy shows that it can actually reduce the amount of effort put toward achieving a goal. This is because our fantasies don't generally call for us to put forth much effort. Things just fall into place.

DISAPPOINTMENT: Engaging in too much fantasy can lead to huge disappointments due to unrealistic expectations. These disappointments can take multiple forms and can be caused by the various ways in which he does not live up to the man in your fantasy.

BLURRED VISION: Engaging in fantasy might blur your vision when a potential suitor comes. You might be in danger of dismissing a potential match because his presentation doesn't exactly match or measure up to the fantasy of him.

On the other hand, visualizing what we want and where we want to be can help us to remain hopeful about the future. Additionally, as the saying goes, "If I can see it, I can be it." However, as with most things in life, moderation is key. Too much fantasy can cause us to distort reality. We can lose touch with reality and begin to prefer the stories we create in our head over the lives that we have the potential to create in reality. One way to help moderate the potential unhealthy impact of fantasy is to focus on yourself rather than on him. Much like the guided imagery exercise in chapter 1, fantasize about you becoming your best self in a relationship. You are the only person whom you can control, change, or improve in order to create the beautiful, fulfilling, and healthy relationship that you desire. Allow images of that version of yourself to fill your fantasy, and allow for "him" to be an ever-evolving figure.

DATING POTENTIAL VERSUS CAPACITY

A close second to the pervasive socialization of being swept off your feet by the fantasy knight is the idea that "a good woman can help a man reach his full potential." Sadly, there is a fundamental flaw in this logic. The flaw rests predominantly in the definition of *potential*. *Merriam-Webster* defines *potential* as "existing in possibility"—that is, the realm of possibility. This means, given the nature of a thing, it *could* become something else. When we apply this logic to human beings, *all* human beings have the potential to become anything that a human being can be. For example, all astronauts are human beings; therefore, any human being has the potential to be an astronaut. Look at it like this: potential means that by being born a living, breathing human, you have the potential to be whatever you want to be. In this case, we all have the potential to be anything. Therefore, potential is a belief founded on an unproven and untested evaluation of possible future behavior. Potential lacks evidence or demonstrations of that ability.

From a "potential" standpoint, we can convince ourselves that he has the potential to be as great as we need him to be. You can follow the word *potential* with "if he" statements to test this logic. "He has the potential to be a great partner if he would stop lying, cheating, and drinking." Potential speaks to an existing deficit, and we often see ourselves as the remedy for the deficit. This is not really the best way to enter a relationship.

Capacity, on the other hand, is defined by *Merriam-Webster* as "an individual's mental or physical ability; aptitude, skill." Capacity is based on demonstrated talent, skill, and ability in a particular area. The judgment of ability is based on the demonstration of the necessary components needed in other areas. Potential without capacity means nothing. He has to demonstrate the capacity, skills, and ability flanked by motivated actions to accomplish the goals and dreams he discusses. You can couple the word *capacity* with "he has" statements: "He has the capacity to make six figures. He has completed all the requirements to go into the management program on his job, has developed a great relationship with his boss, and has received excellent reviews for the past three years." Capacity speaks to existing skills, behaviors, and actions necessary to be what has been stated/observed.

Dating with purpose necessitates a move from dating potential to dating capacity. It is much easier for people to talk about what they want or who they would like to be than it is to put in the work to achieve it. The development of a healthy relationship requires that you stay grounded in reality—the reality of who he is, as he is before you now, not the fantasy of who he *could* become. This doesn't mean that people can't grow and change. It means that we can't date someone with the preformed agenda to change them. Entering a relationship from this place sets the foundation for problems and disappointment.

Note: It is important to be attentive to actions that demonstrate a capacity to engage in both desired and undesirable behaviors.

Here are three questions you can use to begin to assess capacity.

1. Has he demonstrated the skills, behaviors, actions, and abilities to do or be X?
2. Do his current actions match what he says he wants/what he says he is working toward?
3. Do I have a history of dating men with "potential"? How will I work to stop?

HEALTHY RELATIONSHIPS

The term healthy relationship is often used in the relational community in juxtaposition to unhealthy relationship. In discussions, use of the term has become a sort of cliché. Rarely is it defined or explained; it is usually thrown out there to describe the ideal interactions that one should have in close/intimate partnerships. But without an explanation of what a healthy relationship is, people are left to define and interpret the term from their own perspective. This is fine if people have experienced the feelings and behaviors that signify healthy relationships. For those who have not, the tainted lens through which they decipher its meaning can leave a lot to be desired. For example, if you have a history of physical abuse, then you might interpret the meaning of a healthy relationship as one where you are not hit. The problem with this definition is that it is very limited and leaves space for the tolerance of many other unhealthy behaviors, such as emotional abuse.

Healthy relationships are relationships in which each person has freedom. They are free to be, to express their individuality, and to experience personal growth. There is mutual respect, trust/honesty, reciprocity, equality, open communication, safety/security, and a genuine investment in the welfare of the other person. In a nutshell, healthy relationships make us feel good about who we are and about our life. Of course, this does not mean that healthy relationships are devoid of disappointments, but they do not make us compromise our dignity, and mutual respect is always maintained.

Read through this list carefully (appendix 2).

❑ Y N	Mutual trust		❑ Y N	Similar values	
❑ Y N	Mutual respect		❑ Y N	Willingness to be vulnerable	
❑ Y N	Have fun together		❑ Y N	Accept the other as he/she is	
❑ Y N	Physical affection		❑ Y N	Similar goals	
❑ Y N	Neither partner tries to "fix" the other		❑ Y N	Have separate interests and identities	
❑ Y N	Treat each other as equals		❑ Y N	Physical attraction	
❑ Y N	Free from personal attacks, name-calling, sarcasm, belittling, and humiliation		❑ Y N	Look out for each other's best interests	
❑ Y N	Rules and boundaries are respected and honored		❑ Y N	There is a balance of closeness and separation	
❑ Y N	Fight fair		❑ Y N	Shared power	
❑ Y N	Opinions are valued		❑ Y N	Ability to maintain sense of self	
❑ Y N	Each person feels responsible for their own happiness and well-being		❑ Y N	Support and encourage each other	
❑ Y N	You feel physically safe, and your partner doesn't force you to have sex or to do things that make you feel uncomfortable.		❑ Y N	Openness to recognizing when the relationship is changing.	
❑ Y N	Each partner feels whole without the other		❑ Y N	Rules and boundaries are clear	
❑ Y N	Communication is open and respectful		❑ Y N	Each partner is able to regulate their emotions	
❑ Y N	Needs and expectations are clearly articulated		❑ Y N	Consistent displays of fondness and admiration	

CHARACTERISTICS OF HEALTHY RELATIONSHIPS

🦋 What feelings and thoughts came up for you as you read through the list?

_____

_____

_____

_____

_____

_____

🦋 Now go back through the list and put a checkmark next to the seven most important characteristics to you.

🦋 Can you envision having a relationship that contains the seven characteristics that you marked?   Yes   No   Maybe

🦋 What evidence do you have that supports your ability to have a relationship that contains the seven characteristics that you marked?

_____

_____

_____

_____

🦋 What evidence do you have that supports your inability to have a relationship that contains the seven characteristics that you marked?

_____

_____

_____

_____

🦋 Using a different-color pen, go back through the list once more and circle Y (yes) or N (no) next to each healthy relationship characteristic that your parents/caregivers displayed in their intimate relationships. Note: If they were in relationships with others, use one pen color for your mother's and one pen color for your father's relationship characteristics.

🦋 Reflect on the similarities and differences in the characteristics of a healthy relationship that you chose as important to you and the ones that you saw growing up. How do they compare? How are they similar? How do they differ? How did what you experienced growing up influence what you consider important now? What challenges have you noticed as far as displaying healthy relationship characteristics in past relationships?

_____

_____

_____

_____

_____

_____

_____

_____

_____

_____

_____

_____

🦋 Write down the characteristics you want to see displayed in your next relationship.

1. _____   6. _____

2. _____   7. _____

3. _____   8. _____

4. _____   9. _____

5. _____   10. _____

VALUES

No woman really wants a man to carry her off; she only wants him to want to do it.

—Elizabeth Peters

Our values are qualities and psychological virtues that are profoundly and meaningfully important to us. When we live in accordance with our values, our outward actions and behaviors match those inward qualities and virtues. Whenever we talk about values, it is important to differentiate values from beliefs. These two words are often used interchangeably but are distinctly different. Beliefs are the convictions that we generally hold to be true, usually without actual proof. They are judgments about ourselves and the world around us, and they are usually generalizations. Beliefs are basically assumptions that we make about ourselves, others, and the world, and our values stem from those beliefs. Values are abstract and dynamic concepts that are intimately related to our needs. Essentially, values describe what we desire or seek to achieve. Those things that we need, that are important to us, or that are missing from our lives are what we value.

EXAMPLES

BELIEFS	VALUES
• Lying is bad • Smart people don't smoke • God created the world • The earth is flat • Blood is thicker than water	• Commitment • Loyalty • Fairness • Equality • Honesty • Charity

Simply put, beliefs are ideas we hold to be true (without proof), and values are those things that are important to us. Before dating, it is helpful to be consciously aware of the values we hold. Let's begin to identify: What inner values do you find imperative?

 First, draw a line through the qualities that are not important to you (appendix 3).

VALUES LIST

Abundance	Curiosity	Maturity
Acceptance	Daring	Meaning
Accomplishment	Decisiveness	Mindfulness
Adaptability	Discipline	Nonconformity
Affection (loving and caring)	Empathy	Obedience
Altruism	Enthusiasm	Open-mindedness
Ambition	Fairness	Optimism
Assertiveness	Family	Passion
Assurance	Fearlessness	Peace
Audacity	Fidelity	Power
Awareness	Flexibility	Practicality
Beauty	Freedom	Rationality
Brilliance	Friendship	Realism
Certainty	Frugality	Reflection
Challenge	Fun	Reliability
Change	Generosity	Reputation
Clarity	Gratitude	Resilience
Commitment	Growth	Resourcefulness
Community	Health	Respect
Compassion	Honesty	Responsibility
Confidence	Imagination	Security
Conformity	Independence	Self-control
Congruency	Individuality	Selflessness
Connection	Influence	Self-reliance
Consciousness	Integrity	Self-respect
Consistency	Intellect	Sensitivity
Control	Intimacy	Sensuality
Conviction	Introspection	Strength
Courage	Intuition	Trust
Creativity	Justice	Truth
Credibility	Kindness	Unity
	Loyalty	Warmth

🦋 Second, go through the list again, circling all the items that are very important to you.

🦋 Now draw lines through the remaining qualities (these are important but not very important).

🦋 Review the qualities that you circled as very important, and select ten qualities that are most important to you.

🦋 Last, rank in order the ten most important values, with number one being your most important value.

1.	6.
2.	7.
3.	8.
4.	9.
5.	10.

🦋 What emotional associations do I have with each of these words?

_____

_____

_____

_____

_____

_____

_____

_____

_____

_____

_____

_____

Ranking: Write the values you identified in the column below. Then circle the frequency with which you exhibit it in your relationships.

VALUE	I CURRENTLY EMBODY THIS VALUE (CIRCLE ONE)		
1.	Absolutely	Somewhat	Rarely
2.	Absolutely	Somewhat	Rarely
3.	Absolutely	Somewhat	Rarely
4.	Absolutely	Somewhat	Rarely
5.	Absolutely	Somewhat	Rarely
6.	Absolutely	Somewhat	Rarely
7.	Absolutely	Somewhat	Rarely
8.	Absolutely	Somewhat	Rarely
9.	Absolutely	Somewhat	Rarely
10.	Absolutely	Somewhat	Rarely

 For the values that I rarely embody, what hinders me?

_____

_____

_____

_____

_____

_____

_____

_____

_____

_____

🦋 What steps can I take to exemplify them in my daily life?

_____

_____

_____

_____

_____

_____

_____

_____

_____

_____

BOUNDARIES ARE NECESSARY

A lot of people misunderstand what boundaries are and why they are an essential part of a healthy relationship. Some feel that boundaries are unnecessary because "he should already know what I want, what I need, and how to act," or "I don't want to appear too controlling," or "I don't want him to get mad at me," and the list goes on. First, he will never be able to read your mind (and if he can, that is a special talent that is very uncommon in humans). Second, healthy boundaries are not about the other person; they are about honoring yourself. Last, the only people who get mad at us for setting boundaries are people who benefit from us not having any. There is power in saying no when you want to say no, and there is power in saying yes when you want to say yes.

Boundaries are what differentiate us from the other person. They are reminders that we have our own wants and needs in the relationship. Additionally, they are limits we set for ourselves that determine what we will or won't participate in. Boundaries are very individual and cannot be compared to the boundaries of others. They are based on your values and what you need/desire in order to feel respected and heard in the relationship.

We can think of boundaries in three ways. Rigid boundaries erect walls and serve to keep others at a distance. Weak boundaries are really the absence of boundaries; they provide no information to others about our limits because we don't demonstrate any. Healthy boundaries are clearly defined limits that are consistently enforced and serve as self-care.

 What do healthy and unhealthy boundaries look like?

HEALTHY BOUNDARIES	UNHEALTHY BOUNDARIES (RIGID BOUNDARIES/WEAK BOUNDARIES)
• You know your limits. • You allow others to define their own limits. • You communicate your needs, wants, and feelings clearly. • You can say no or yes, and you can tolerate hearing no from others. • You are responsible for your happiness and allow others to be responsible for their happiness. • You don't compromise your values or integrity to avoid rejection.	• You take on others' problems as your own (weak). • Your requests are more like demands (rigid). • You can't say no because you are afraid of rejection or abandonment (weak). • You'd rather be right than happy (rigid). • You allow others to define your limits (weak). • You often come off as cold and unavailable (rigid). • You try to define the limits of others (weak). • You compromise your values and beliefs in order to please others or avoid conflict (weak).

In addition to the broader categories of healthy and unhealthy boundaries, there are specific areas where boundaries are necessary.

Here are a few examples:

- **Personal:** I do not allow people to come to my house without calling first.

- **Emotional:** I don't feel comfortable talking about the death of my mother just now.

- **Mental:** I prefer not to talk about politics at work.

- **Material:** Please do not go through my cell phone without asking.

- **Physical:** I don't like to be grabbed from behind.

Some of us have an easier time setting boundaries with some people versus others. For example, we may have very clearly defined healthy boundaries at work, but we might have difficulty creating them within families or intimate relationships. Helping you to fix your weak boundaries with your mother is beyond the scope of this book, but it is important to know that having weak boundaries in intimate relationships can have devastating impacts. Unhealthy boundaries in dating relationships can lead to feelings of disrespect and unmet needs, even to extreme situations such as abuse.

In order to establish boundaries, you need to be clear with your partner about who you are, what you want and don't want, what you value, and your limits. Boundaries are very individual and cannot be compared to the boundaries of others. They are based on your values and what you need/desire in order to feel respected and heard in the relationship. Boundaries that are too rigid or too vague don't work.

Use this exercise to create simple boundary statements that can be used to communicate a clear message to your partner about your needs. Remember that you can have multiple boundaries in each area; however, for this exercise, only list one per area. We don't want to run the risk of creating a laundry list of rigid rules to control him. In this exercise use the ten values that you identified in chapter 5 to help you to develop statements that align with your values.

AREA	BOUNDARY STATEMENT
Personal	
Emotional	
Mental	
Material	
Physical	

What difficulties have I had setting healthy boundaries in previous relationships?

_____

_____

_____

_____

_____

_____

_____

_____

_____

Three things I can do to increase my ability to begin to set healthy boundaries.

1. _____

2. _____

3. _____

I WANT THAT: FOUR-SQUARE PLAN

Don't look for a partner who is eye candy. Look for a partner who is soul food.

—*Karen Salmansohn*

We have spent the past chapters reflecting on your past. Now it is time to begin to plan for your future. Knowing what we want and need from a relationship will help us evaluate potential suitors relatively quickly. Let's begin by distinguishing between what you "want" versus what you "need." To help you to tell the difference, I have divided these two categories into four subcategories. Essentials and Dealbreakers describe the things that you need, and Negotiables and Doesn't Matter are more like wants. The following descriptions should help you understand the differences between each.

ESSENTIALS should be connected to internal characteristics, not more-superficial traits. There's a difference between Essentials and preferences. Superficial things like hair color, height, style of dress, and so on are all considered preferences. I call preferences superficial not because they are not important but because they are often not eternal. These things tend to change over time. The body eventually fades, hair color changes, we even get shorter as we age. There is nothing wrong with having preferences, but there is an important distinction. Preferences are things that you like; Essentials should be things you can't live without. Must-haves should be connected to his internal traits and characteristics. These are the things that are basically stable across time and are essential for a true intimate connection with another.

Review your values earlier in the chapter. These should be the basis for your Essentials.

DEALBREAKERS are your walk-aways. This list should be relatively short and should include behaviors that you will not tolerate. This should not be a list of threats, nor should they be bluffs. Also, these should not be used to manipulate your partner into doing what you want him to do. This list should contain only the item/items that will make you walk away from him and from the relationship. For example, abuse of any kind is a good way to begin your Dealbreakers list (see appendix 4 to better understand the faces of abuse/power and the control wheel). Dealbreakers and boundaries should be clearly communicated to your date. It is important for him to know your expectations immediately, which gives him an opportunity to decide whether he is willing to respect your parameters.

Review your values on page earlier in this chapter. These should be the basis for your Dealbreakers.

NEGOTIABLES are items that you are open to compromising on. These are most closely related to preferences. Negotiables are things that you desire, but it won't kill you if he doesn't show up with them. Recognize that there is a difference between negotiable/compromise and settling. You never negotiate your boundaries or values.

DOESN'T MATTER are the things that others might have told you are important for a relationship but, when you think about it, don't really matter to you. For example, you don't care about the old social norm that he has to make more money than you or if he wants to stay home with the kids.

Take a moment to reflect on each category. Take your time and begin to fill in items in each category. Think about the importance of each item and why you are putting it in the specific category. Once completed, review it forty-eight hours later and make any revisions that you might want to make after you look at it with fresh eyes.

FOUR-SQUARE PLAN (APPENDIX 5)

ESSENTIALS (VALUES)	DEALBREAKERS (BOUNDARIES)
(example: must want children)	*(example: verbal, physical, or emotional abuse)*

NEGOTIABLES (COMPROMISES)	DOESN'T MATTER (UNIMPORTANT)
(example: relocation)	*(example: college degree)*

DATING IN RAPID SUCCESSION

Dating with purpose means that you are dating with a plan, being focused and deliberate. You know what you want, how you want to be treated, and what you won't go for. You are committed to dating with a balance between your head and your heart. This means that you need to avoid becoming prematurely emotionally attached. You must limit time and interaction until you begin to see that this is worth the investment. The idea is for it not to take three years to figure out that this relationship is not the one. I have worked with many women who find themselves back on the dating scene after spending two, four, even ten years in a relationship that they knew was unhealthy in the second month of dating. We've already explored this phenomenon in chapters 2 and 4. Just because he's confused about what he wants presently doesn't mean that you have to waste your time waiting. Besides, when he does decide what he wants, it might not be you.

The first step to dating in rapid succession is to assess a potential partner based on your Four-Square Plan. Does he possess your Essentials? Do any red flags signal Dealbreakers on the horizon?

The second step to dating in rapid succession is knowing when it is time to let go. This requires that you develop the ability to rapidly assess the potential of a new prospect. Let's begin by reading the signs.

Seven Signs that It's Time to Go

 He has difficulty with consistent communication.

 You catch him in "little white lies."

 You doubt many things about him, the relationship, and/or yourself.

 His values are very different from yours.

His emotional health is questionable: he is self-absorbed, overly defensive, easily angered, and is unwilling to actively seek and participate in treatment.

You're making excuses and/or justifying his behavior. Either or both mean that you are lying to yourself.

He is often missing in action, non-responsive, or disappears for days on end and then pops up with a "What you doing?" text.

The third step to dating in rapid succession is to be honest with yourself. Why are you entertaining him as a potential? Review your answers in chapter 4. Commit to making a conscious decision to stay or leave.

Chapter 5 Reflection

What did I learn about myself in this chapter?

_____

_____

_____

_____

_____

_____

_____

_____

_____

_____

_____

_____

_____

_____

How will my future dating behaviors change as a result of this chapter?

_____

_____

_____

_____

_____

_____

_____

_____

_____

_____

What am I specifically committed to do, moving forward?

_____

_____

_____

_____

_____

_____

_____

_____

_____

_____

_____

_____

🦋   What skills and tools will I use from this chapter?

_____

_____

_____

_____

_____

_____

_____

_____

_____

_____

_____

_____

_____

_____

6

Getting Out There: Rules of Engagement

You can make your own way. It's about getting out
there and not letting rejection get you down.

—Jennifer Armentrout

I know that getting back into the dating scene is not as easy as it sounds. However, it is virtually impossible to date, much less date with purpose, without putting yourself in places to be seen. Unless he is the package-delivery guy, a door-to-door salesman, or the gardener, he is not likely to show up on your doorstep. Yes, there are many reasons that actively engaging in meeting people might be a challenge for you. Maybe you don't get out much because of work or finances, or you consider yourself a homebody. Maybe you simply hate the club scene, or there is a lack of a club scene in your town. You might have family obligations that leave you with little free time. Maybe emotional reasons such as being shy, introverted, socially awkward, or fearful impact the way that you move about the world. Although this workbook is not designed to address nor eliminate these real-life barriers to actively being seen, it can help you explore barriers to successful dating and expand options and get you prepared to step out.

THE "F" WORD

If you want to conquer fear, don't sit home and
think about it. Go out and get busy.

—*Dale Carnegie*

It can be scary to think about getting back on the dating scene if you've been away for a while or if you've had bad experiences in the past. Even if you haven't taken an official hiatus, whether deliberate or circumstantial, it can be frightening to think about dating with purpose. In talking to women across the United States, I have found that the bases for their fears are as diverse as the women themselves. Some have a fear of rejection, others have a fear of meeting somebody "crazy," and some have a fear of being labeled "desperate" or "easy." I want to take time to address each of these briefly.

FEAR OF REJECTION: The fear of rejection often comes from the anticipation of feelings of embarrassment and hurt feelings that result from someone not "liking" you. This often leads to negative, self-deprecating thoughts, such as "I am not good enough" or "I'll never find anyone." One way to decrease this fear is to change the way you think about "rejection," which will help to change the resulting feelings that may develop. I see rejection as a natural part of dating. You will be rejected and, if you are dating with your head and your heart, will also reject others. First, let's not use the word rejection. Let's use the term not a good match. Next, let's think about this logically: you will never be a perfect match for every guy you date, and every guy you date will not be a perfect match for you. Isn't it better that you find out you are not a good match for each other so that you both can move on? In essence, when a guy tells you that you two are not a good match for each other, he is freeing you up to find the one. Hmm—in that case, rejection is actually opportunity. It doesn't mean anything about your desirability, your mate-ability, or your worth. Each occurrence opens the door for Mr. Right.

FEAR OF MEETING SOMEBODY "CRAZY": Well, yes, there are people out there who have ulterior motives or bad intentions. And a healthy dose of fear can keep you on your toes. But fear that is paralyzing is counterproductive. The reality is that there are bad people everywhere, and these people can be both men and women. Therefore, it is important for you to be wise when meeting anyone new. I talk about strategies in the next section. There are precautions that you can take to increase your safety when dating.

FEAR OF BEING LABELED "DESPERATE" OR "EASY": This was covered in chapter 1, and I hope, after completing the first five chapters, that you know that chasing men down in the streets is not the purpose of your action. Dating with purpose is about using your head and your heart, developing strategies to prepare yourself for dating, and actively engaging in strategies to increase the quality of your dating life. Dating with purpose is the exact opposite of desperation.

Research shows that fear is a healthy and necessary emotion. Experiencing some fear increases our caution, makes us more mindful, and serves to keep us safe. However, when fear becomes overwhelming, it can paralyze us and prevent us from engaging in even normal parts of life.

Reflection

🦋 When thinking about getting back out there, my fears are:

_____

_____

_____

_____

_____

_____

_____

_____

_____

_____

_____

🦋 How has fear impacted my dating life?

_____

_____

_____

_____

_____

_____

_____

_____

_____

_____

_____

_____

_____

🦋 What is my evidence that my fear is true?

_____

_____

_____

_____

_____

_____

_____

_____

_____

_____

🦋 What is my evidence that my fear is untrue?

_____

_____

_____

_____

_____

_____

_____

_____

_____

_____

_____

🦋 What can I do to reduce the potential for what I fear to come true?

_____

_____

_____

_____

_____

_____

_____

_____

_____

_____

🦋 What can I do to reduce the impact that my fear has on my dating life?

_____

_____

_____

_____

_____

_____

_____

_____

_____

_____

_____

_____

RULES OF ENGAGEMENT

As you prepare to get back out there, first you need to understand the rules of engagement. Dating with purpose requires that you go into each encounter thoughtfully and with clear intentions. This will require some of you to acquire new skills and ideas around dating. For others, this will be a reminder of what you already know but might not do consistently. Remember, dating always begins with safety first and ends with a good assessment.

◆🧩 RULE 1: SAFETY FIRST.

Your safety should always be your number-one priority. Keeping yourself and your loved ones safe should be at the forefront of your mind whenever you begin to invite strangers into your world. Unfortunately, there are people out there who don't have good intentions and who move through the world as predators. Remember that predators are always on the prowl for prey. Yes, I know that this can sound like doom and gloom, and many of us desire to see the inherent "good" in everyone; however, we have to acknowledge that some people have been so damaged by their lived experiences (family of origin, peers, other predators, etc.) that the good is buried deep, deep inside and can only be excavated by a trained professional under strict conditions. In the absence of that, they move through the world inflicting their internal pain outwardly onto anyone that they lure into their web. This realization is not meant to scare you but to urge you to have a healthy amount of skepticism and well-defined boundaries.

Also understand that being cautious does not equate to being paranoid; it's smart.

Here is a list of fifteen things that you should do for at least the first three dates with every suitor.

Yes, you read right, the *first three dates*! Of course, this list is not exhaustive, but it gives you a place to begin. For those of you who have more expertise in these areas, I have included maven tips to kick it up a notch.

1. **Make all your social media accounts private.**

   So much of our world today revolves around social media and sharing our lives with the world. I am sure you've heard the dangers with this, so I won't belabor the point. Just know that the more information you post for the world to see, the easier it is to find information you didn't want to disclose.

Maven tip: Never lie, but commit to being vague. For example, if the site asks for your occupation, use the major category rather than the specific job title. If you are a social worker, you can say that you work in a helping profession.

2. **Do not provide your first and last name.**

   This includes trying to impress him by providing your business card. Similar to the first tip, the more information he has about you, the easier it is to find your personal information.

Maven tip: Even if you meet someone in person, only give your first name, and don't say your first and last name on your voicemail.

3. **Do your own online mini investigation.**

   Yup, I am urging you to do to him the exact thing that I am trying to teach you not to allow him to do to you. A little internet sleuthing can provide you some insight into those parts of his life that he has not disclosed to you yet. It couldn't hurt, right?

Maven tip: Search both names and images. Many major search engines have this ability.

4. **Google yourself.**

   Are you Googleable? Have you searched your first and last name to see what and how much information comes up on the internet? If not, put a reminder in your phone to do this at least once per year. Remember, if you can find him, he can find you.

Maven tip: Look yourself up using multiple browsers (e.g., Google, Explorer, Firefox). Also ask a few friends to look you up to see if their search turns up something different.

5. **Meet rather than ride together.**

   Securing your own transportation provides a layer of safety and also offers freedom. Not only does it eliminate the potential to be locked in the car with a complete stranger, but it also ensures that you can leave when you desire. Be sure to preplan your solo ride home as well.

Maven tip: Arrive early to get a parking space close to the venue so you won't have to walk far away from the building when you're leaving.

6. **You pick the place.**

   It is never a good idea to meet a stranger in a strange place. It's important for your first few dates to be in a place you are familiar with—ideally, with folks you are at least somewhat familiar with. You don't have to go to a place where everybody knows your name, but someone there should at least recognize your face.

Maven tip: Select a small restaurant or coffee shop. There is more of a likelihood that workers will keep an eye on you.

7. **Tell friends.**

   Always provide detailed information to at least two other folks when going on a date. This should include the date's name, where you're going, time you're expected to return, and any other information that will help them identify him.

   Maven tip: Text your friend a picture of him, if you have one.

8. **Let him know that you have done step 7.**

   It is important for him to know that you are connected to other people and that others are aware of him. His reaction can also give you insight into whether he might be hiding something.

   Maven tip: Ask him, "How does it make you feel for me to tell you that?"

9. **Have your friend call you during the date, and agree to call them when you are back home safely.**

   Stay in contact with someone during the date. This lets him know that you are connected and that someone knows where you are, who you are with, and when you are expected to return. This can also give you a sense of not being alone with a stranger.

   Maven tip: Create code words for "things are good" and "I'm concerned."

10. **Don't drink alcohol at all, or at the very least limit alcohol consumption.**

Alcohol impairs judgment, and when dating with purpose your judgment is crucial. Alcohol also has a tendency to reduce inhibitions, which can be dangerous in a number of ways.

Maven tip: *Pick a place that doesn't even serve alcohol.*

11. **Never leave food or beverages unattended.**

There are multiple drugs available currently that are odorless and colorless that, when ingested, will make you disoriented or unconscious. They are commonly referred to as "date-rape" drugs for a reason. We don't want to believe that someone we're on a date with will slip us any drugs, but it does happen. Don't accept a drink from your date unless you open it yourself or watch it being prepared by a bartender.

Maven tip: *Use the restroom before your date starts. This should eliminate the need to leave the table once you're served.*

12. **Keep the dates to a specified time limit.**

This guarantees that your date will have a definite beginning and end. It reduces the need for you to come up with an awkward or forced end. Further, it eliminates the potential for the date to end at somebody's place in somebody's bed.

Maven tip: *A lunch date during the workweek is often perfect because you both have time constraints.*

13. **Leave if you begin to feel uncomfortable.**

   Don't feel obligated to stay. If you feel compelled to stay and you are less than three dates in, you will probably be reluctant to leave an unhealthy relationship at four months in. You have your own cell phone, money, and transportation (#5, #14). You are in a familiar place (#6), and others know where you are (#7, #9). Additionally, he doesn't know where you live or work (#1 through #4).

Maven tip: Tell the waiter, barista, hostess, or owner that you are on a first date and that you feel uncomfortable. Ask them to keep an eye on you as you walk to your car.

14. **Take the essentials.**

   At minimum this includes your wallet with enough money to pay for your meal or coffee if need be, your cell phone, and a little valve of pepper spray.

Maven tip: Keep the location service enabled on your cell phone. This will give folks a way to find you if you need to be found.

15. **Don't go out with him if he objects to any of the tips above.**

   A true gentleman will respect your boundaries, understand that as a woman you are vulnerable, and be invested in your safety. He would also want you to be safe; want to show that he can tolerate delayed gratification or put his own desires in check; and have a desire to make you comfortable.

Maven tip: A man who wants to protect you without being controlling is often a plus.

SAFETY CHECKLIST AND PLAN (APPENDIX 6)

TASK	DETAILS	✓
1. Social media account privacy setting		
2. Online screen name		
3. Internet search (him)		
4. Internet search (me)		
5. How will I get there?		
6. First-date places		
7. Friends I will notify about my dates		
8. When will I tell him that I've taken these precautions?		
9. This friend will call while I'm on the date:		
10. My nonalcoholic beverages will be:		
11. How will I ensure that my food/drink is not left unattended?		
12. Days of the week that are usually good for (lunch) dates		
13. I commit to leaving if I become uncomfortable.		

14. Make sure I have:
    Money
    Cell phone
    Pepper spray
    Key-chain alarm		

15. I have done steps 1 through 14.		

RULE 2: DON'T MOVE TOO FAST.

In this microwave world, we frequently want instant gratification and rewards. Unfortunately, this strategy doesn't often work when dating to find a meaningful and lasting relationship. Take your time and commit to getting to know him and yourself (with him). There are no universal dating timelines that will ensure the success of your relationship. If you talk to a hundred women in committed relationships, they will probably tell you a hundred different scenarios about the progression of their relationship. However, when dating with purpose, remember that the objective is to date with both your head and your heart. Therefore, your goal is to maintain a balance between what you know and what you feel. The pace at which you do that is highly dependent on you. Nevertheless, I do have a few suggestions.

There should be three successful dates that follow the safety-first rules before you're allowed to depart from those precautions. The safety rules were designed to help provide dating boundaries that require the head to be engaged, from the planning to the ending of the date. Giving yourself more time to think with a clear head and assess the potential for this to succeed in meeting the goal in chapter 1 is the whole point.

Be mindful of engaging in long, deep phone/texting conversations multiple times per day. This is a slippery slope. First, the more contact you have, the more contact you'll desire. Your heart will begin to long for the call, the affirming text, the connection, which is an unquestionably natural human response. But your heart can convince your mind that you are in "like" with him when you are really in "love" with the attention/company. Second, when you have constant communication over the phone, through texting, or even on the internet, there is a tendency to develop a false sense of familiarity and knowing. There is the danger of a first date feeling like a fifth, leading you not to be as vigilant about getting to know the guy in front of you versus the one on the other end of the line/keyboard.

RULE 3: EVERYONE AIN'T THE ONE.

If you are thinking about your wedding dress as you get ready for your first date, please cancel the date. As I stressed in chapter 1, dating with purpose should be a thoughtful, fun exploration of potential mates. It should not be a last resort of the desperate. If you enter into a date already believing that he is the one, you will reek of desperation. This could negatively impact a natural progression of connection. There is less probability that you will put your thinking cap on. And he might see you as needy or an easy conquest (which for many men is a turnoff). Most men need a conquest, and if you've already decided that he's the one, there is nothing for him to conquer, chase, or win over.

![puzzle] RULE 4: DON'T COMPROMISE YOUR VALUES OR INTEGRITY.

Remember your stated values in chapter 5, and know when you are considering actions that are not in line with your morals and values. Hold strong to the beliefs that you prize.

![puzzle] RULE 5: RED FLAGS ARE INEVITABLE.

Red flags are commonly defined as early warning signs that there might be a larger problem lying beneath the surface. Red flags are not necessarily stop signs or red lights but are more like flashing yellow lights or a yield sign. You can't cut and run every time you see a red flag. We are all flawed—yes, even you, remember? Therefore, red flags should be areas for further investigation or evaluation by exploration. *If you see too many red flags flying high, you might want to look for love elsewhere even if the chemistry is of nuclear proportion.*

Here are some common red flags to watch for:

 He talks down to you.

Talking down to you includes talking with a sense of superiority or an air of arrogance. You begin to feel self-conscious or less-than when interacting with him. He might make critical comments about who you are, what you've done, how you've done it, and what you think, et cetera. These criticisms might be direct or delivered with humor. But either way, *it is a little too biting.*

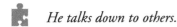 *He talks down to others.*

He might be nice and polite to you, but he is rude, dismissive, or downright aggressive to others. While you are on your date, he belittles or berates the server, parking attendant, or other patrons. He suffers from road rage (you hear this while talking on the phone because you haven't been in his car yet).

 You seem more interested/invested than he is.

Is the relationship reciprocal? Realistically, it might be impossible for there to be a fifty-fifty split. Beware if you begin to initiate the majority of the contact, conversation, or enthusiasm.

 He is inconsistent.

Inconsistency can show up in at least two ways. First, are his statements consistent from one conversation to the next? In one conversation he says, "I haven't dated in about six months," then two conversations later he says his ex has been stalking him ever since they broke up last month. Initially, I like to call these "verbal inconsistencies," until they prove themselves to be willful lies. Keep your ears open. Second, are there inconsistencies in what he does? Does he call or text every day for four days and then become completely unavailable for two days (without warning)?

 He talks about changing you.

"Oh, you're going to feel so great once I get you to change to a vegan lifestyle" or "You know, I always pictured myself with a woman who has short hair." Statements like this are not about who you are but about who he wants you to be. There is a difference between stating a preference and going into a relationship with a "change" agenda. This is not to say that you shouldn't be introduced to new things; this is one of the most exciting aspects of getting to know new people. However, it is important for your prospect to accept you for who you are and what you bring to the table, and if they do have a helpful suggestion, then you saying "no thank you" should be a real option without penalty (remember your boundaries).

 He ignores your boundaries.

Honoring your boundaries is not only a sign of respect but also shows that he has the ability to put someone else's needs before his own. If he pressures you to do things that you have previously stated you do not want to do, he might have difficulty honoring your needs. You must also be consistent with your boundaries to ensure that you are not sending confusing messages. For example, if you state, "I am not comfortable coming to your place yet," but every time that you communicate with him he is asking you to meet him at his house, that should raise an eyebrow—and a concern.

 He has a drama narrative.

A drama narrative is when he tells you story after story about the drama that is occurring in his life. The drama could be in the form of conflict with family, coworkers, and/or friends, and then there's a story about how his car was impounded last week because he forgot to pay a parking ticket, his bank account was hacked, and he's in a phone dispute with the water-delivery guy because his water was delivered to his neighbor's house. Now each of these situations by themselves could happen to anyone, but if they are happening at the same time or all the time, constant chaos might be his normal way of life. Even if it is not, he might not be in a position to focus on dating right now because his focus is on putting out fires.

 He doesn't talk about or doesn't want you to meet his friends or family.

I am not suggesting that you make plans to meet his people three dates in. But if he never mentions his family, friends, or other important people in his life, that should raise a question or two. It is important for him to demonstrate that he has a history of establishing and maintaining relationships. If he has limited contact with his family, in all honesty that might be a healthy decision if the family is toxic, but has he developed close friendships and a support system? As with all red flags, this alone might not have a deeper meaning. Then again, it might.

 He asks you for money.

Unless you have dedicated yourself to a life of philanthropy, never, ever give money to a guy that you're just getting to know. One has to wonder why he needs money from you. There could be many reasons, none of which are your responsibility. This request should raise questions about his money-management skills, as well as why he doesn't have other established relationships that he can depend on when he's in a bind (i.e., has he burned bridges before over money and now his friends are not open to lending anymore?). Regardless of the answers to these questions, giving money to a man that you are getting to know can set up a very bad precedent.

RED FLAG CHECKLIST (APPENDIX 7)   ✓

1. Does he seem too good to be true? ☐
2. Does he say, "Let's be friends first" but doesn't respect personal space and sexual boundaries? ☐
3. Does he send sexual or nude pictures or ask for them? ☐
4. Does he have an addiction, whether substance (alcohol, drugs) or behavior (gambling, porn), that he refuses to get help for because "it is not a problem"? ☐
5. Is he married or otherwise unavailable to be in a committed relationship right now? ☐
6. Does he no-show for dates? ☐
7. Does he talk about his past relationships a lot? ☐
8. Does conversation often revolve around him (what he's doing, what he needs, what he likes, what he wants, what he thinks, etc.)? ☐
9. Is he standoffish, shallow, or emotionally distant? ☐
10. Is his behavior inconsistent or changing often? ☐
11. Is he rude or disrespectful toward you or others? ☐
12. Does he lack integrity in dealing with things (honesty, money) or people? ☐
13. Does he have a quick fuse and react to frustration with extreme anger or blame? ☐
14. Does he have difficulty accepting responsibility? Is it always someone else's fault? ☐
15. Is his life unstable or filled with drama or things that need to be "worked out" (whether it's his fault or not)? ☐

Add your own:

16. ☐
17. ☐

◀▓▶ RULE 6: DON'T WASTE YOUR TIME.

*Dating is primarily a numbers game . . . People usually go through a
lot of people to find good relationships. That's just the way it is.*

—Henry Cloud

Dating with purpose means that you are dating with the desire to find a guy with whom a
healthy, committed relationship has the likelihood to blossom. Don't hang around if you know
that it's not right. This means that you are not dating for nine, twelve, or eighteen months to
confirm what you knew six weeks after you met. Research shows that couples who make it to
three months usually end up together for at least four years. This goes for both healthy and
unhealthy relationships. So the three-month mark is an important milestone. The longer you
stay, the more likely he is to become a "habit," a part of your daily routine (i.e., the morning
texts, the late-night calls). You then begin to expect, even long for, the interaction, and before
you know it, the habit is felt and interpreted as an emotional connection. Once you're emotionally invested, it will become harder to walk away. Additionally, the longer you stay in a
relationship that is not meeting your purpose, the longer you are off the market and are not
available for the right one to find yourself.

Add Your Own

◀▓▶ RULE 7:

_____

_____

_____

_____

_____

_____

⚙ RULE 8:

_____

_____

_____

_____

_____

_____

_____

_____

_____

_____

Chapter 6 Reflection

🦋 What came up for me as I read this chapter?

_____

_____

_____

_____

_____

_____

_____

_____

_____

_____

_____

_____

_____

🦋 Which rules of engagement will be most difficult for me to follow?

_____

_____

_____

_____

_____

_____

_____

_____

_____

_____

_____

_____

🦋 What will I do to increase my chances of following the rules?

_____

_____

_____

_____

_____

_____

_____

_____

_____

_____

_____

_____

_____

🦋 What skills and tools did I learn in this chapter?

_____

_____

_____

_____

_____

_____

_____

_____

_____

_____

_____

_____

_____

7

Where Is He?

*It's always fun when you get to go somewhere new and you
get to meet new people and get new experiences.*

—J. B. Bickerstaff

MEET UP OR HOOK UP

There are many ways that people meet, and not every option is feasible for everyone. Although I cannot tell you where to meet him, I can tell you that you won't meet him sitting in your house alone every night after work catching up on your latest reality show. You will only meet him by reducing your time watching reality television and increasing your time living in reality. If you are not meeting any potential men doing the things that you normally do, then it is time for you to do something differently if you want a different outcome. I am not suggesting that you go hunt him down. I am suggesting, however, that you must put yourself in situations that increase the likelihood that you and he will share the same space. For example, if you said, "I really want to swim in the ocean on my vacation," but then booked a ticket to Arizona, your chances of feeling the warm waters of the Atlantic or the cool waters of the Pacific are slim to none. However, when you think about the things he would enjoy or appreciate, you may determine where to find him. Perhaps your Mr. Right is a fan of jazz—maybe visiting some cozy jazz clubs would lead you to him. By knowing what you're looking for, you'll determine how to find him.

PICK ONE OR TWO OR THREE

What follows are suggestions. These are all suggestions, and not all suggestions are good options for all women. This list is not exhaustive either. These are simply samples and suggested ways that you can use to expand your dating pool.

◆ Tell a friend/get hooked up.

> *When friends introduced us, I said "Hi"—and turned my back. Later, I called my mom and best friend and said, "I think I just met my wife."*
>
> —*Mike Vogel*

Your friends can be untapped sources of potential mates. Think about it logically. The likelihood that people in the same social circle share similar interests and values is very high, which can foster an early connection. Research consistently shows that the majority of married couples report meeting through mutual friends (although there has been a sharp rise in the number of people who met via online dating over the last five years, it hasn't caught up yet). This does not strictly mean being set up by friends but includes things like meeting friends of friends at social gatherings, work functions, or social media connections.

There are several reasons we don't tell our friends that we are actively dating. Shame, fear of looking desperate, not wanting to be the topic of gossip, wanting to keep your personal life private, not believing there are any potentials, et cetera. Let's not minimize the factors that prevent you from disclosing to friends in this way. It can be a risk, and risks are scary. Additionally, you have to be mindful of how your initial friendship might change or be affected by the mutual relationship.

🦋 Is dating friends of friends an option for me? Why or why not?

_____

_____

_____

_____

_____

_____

_____

_____

🦋 If I were to make myself open to dating friends of friends, how would I approach it? What would I do specifically? What friends do I believe would have the best chance of having potentials in their circle?

_____

_____

_____

_____

_____

_____

_____

_____

_____

◀▓ Online dating.

Online dating is just as murky and full of lemons as finding a
used car in the classifieds. Once you learn the lingo, it's easier
to spot the models with high mileage and no warranty.

—*Laurie Perry*

A recent study found that close to 40 percent of Americans have used online dating sites. The creation of new online dating apps, the convenience of smartphones, and the decrease in stigma have all contributed to this increase. There are many online dating sites, and, in my experience, each site has its own "culture." I have heard many women say that they hate online dating or that they tried it and it wasn't successful. That's like saying, "I went to a clothing store and tried on the clothes, I didn't find anything that I liked, so shopping in clothing stores is not an option for me." In the same way that not all clothing stores are alike, neither are online dating sites. You have your high-end sites, your specialty sites, your discount sites, your local boutique sites, et cetera. I am not telling you that you should try online dating; I am merely suggesting that you do your own research and make an informed decision about whether online dating could be an additional option. And we all know that the more options you have, the greater the pool from which you can choose.

🦋 Is online dating an option for me? Why or why not?

_____

_____

_____

_____

_____

_____

_____

Do your own internet research of online dating sites. Record pertinent information for your reference.

ONLINE DATING PLAN

DATING SITE NAME	TARGET AUDIENCE	PRICE	NOTES

Meet-ups and other social-interest groups

Life is what happens when you're busy making other plans.

—Allen Saunders

Getting involved in interest groups can be a fun and exciting way to get back out there. Meet-ups are a wonderful way to be in the company of people who have similar interests. This can provide an opportunity to break up the monotony of your usual routine and give you a chance to meet new people, and you might also learn a new skill (depending on the group you attend). I recommend you find a group that matches your interests and provides the most opportunity for you to interact with the other participants.

🦋 Are meet-ups or social-interest groups an option for me? Why or why not?

_____

_____

_____

_____

_____

_____

_____

_____

_____

🦋 Do online research about meet-ups and other activities in your city. Which groups spark your interest?

_____

_____

_____

_____

_____

_____

_____

_____

_____

_____

_____

_____

_____

_____

_____

❖ While doing daily duties: gym, gas station, grocery store, movie theater

*The remarkable thing is we have a choice every day regarding
the attitude we will embrace for that day.*

—Charles R. Swindoll

Daily errands are often an opportunity to meet someone new. It is also the most random approach, similar to playing the slot machine. The fact is, when you run errands they are usually within your community and part of your routine. By doing the same thing consistently, the likelihood is that you will continually run into the same people. All of you are engaged in a routine, and the chances of a new person being at the cleaners at the very time that you are is slim. However, although it might be a long shot, you should always be prepared, because you could just hit the jackpot.

Preparation includes pulling yourself together, at least somewhat, when leaving the house. I am not saying that you need to put on your prom dress and five-inch heels to go to Starbucks, but you can wash your face, brush your hair, and put on clean and matching sweats and T-shirt. Remember, men are very visual. Interest is piqued with their eyes first. No matter your body type, hair color, bone structure, there is someone for you, but it is difficult for them to see you if you look like you just rolled out of bed to get a loaf of bread. You can argue about how superficial this is until the cows come home, but it doesn't change the fact that if you walk around like you've been rode hard and put away wet, you will turn a lot of heads—but for the wrong reasons.

❖ Stop rolling ten deep.

Sometimes your circle decreases in size but increases in value.

—Unknown

I know that hanging with a group of girlfriends can be a great time. They provide company, a shoulder, validation, commiseration, et cetera. And they also provide a major roadblock to meeting a potential. Most men are just as afraid of rejection on the dating scene as women are. They are even more afraid of being rejected in front of a group of women who will be sizing a man up from the first step that he takes toward you all. A group of women can feel like a virtual cement wall to an interested guy. Please don't say that "If he was secure," "If he was a man," "If he was confident in himself," he would . . . Please cut that out. This has nothing to do with confidence; it has to do with common sense. You know that doing anything in front of a group of people is more intimidating than doing that thing in front of one or two people. Whether it is a job interview, an audition, karaoke, or stepping out of a fitting room, they all feel better with fewer eyes on you. So why would you judge a man's confidence by his ability to brave the glares of twenty bright eyes sizing him up and intently judging your response? When dating with purpose, keep your road crew to no more than two or three of you. Remember, it is all about increasing your potential!

 Let's plan ahead.

ACTIVITY	FRIEND TO INVITE	BACKUP FRIEND

MY BEST SELF

When you get out there, it is important to present the best version of yourself. There is a difference between creating a false self and being your best self. A false self is the equivalent of wearing a mask to disguise who you really are. Whether intentionally or unintentionally, when you present a false self you behave dishonestly. Additionally, you deprive others from getting to know the real you, and you deprive yourself of being liked for who you are. When you commit to be the best version of yourself, you commit to let your light shine. You determine to be you in all the best ways possible. You will be your best mentally, physically, and spiritually. You will look your best, you will smell your best, you will speak your best, you will feel your best, you will do your best. You might say, "But I am not my best self every day, so if I show up as my best self now, is that being honest?" To that I say, the major difference is that the best version of yourself is just enhancing what you have naturally. This enhancement can be re-created daily, weekly, yearly, or on special occasions. At least this way you make purposeful effort for him to see you at your best, because if it turns into a long-term relationship, he is guaranteed to see you at your worst at some point—like when you catch the flu or when you feel down because of something bad happening or when you wake up in the morning with bed head. Being your best self encompasses the characteristics below.

CONFIDENCE: If you do not believe in yourself, no one else will. You must believe that you are lovable, that you are valuable, and that your one is out there. If you truly internalize these beliefs, they will radiate from your being. You will carry yourself differently, you will engage with others differently, and you will attract others differently. Being confident is not the same as being arrogant. Confidence comes from within; it is an internalized belief in yourself. On the other hand, arrogance is more about a need for external validation and is often a mask for low self-confidence. Be aware that there are some men who are threatened by a woman with confidence.

LOOKS: The way you look can impact your confidence. For some, when they have on their favorite outfit, they feel more confident. For others, when they feel confident, they select clothes that personify that feeling. Any way you look at it, it is safe to say that it is a cyclical relationship. However, looking your best is not about dressing like a supermodel; it is about working with what you have and loving it.

HYGIENE: Many of you are probably rolling your eyes at this one. No one needs to tell you about your hygiene. For you, this is stating the obvious. Even if this is the case, could you just humor me by reading the following three sentences (I promise you, someone needs to hear this). Presenting your best self includes taking time to engage in daily grooming and hygiene practices. Perfume never replaces a shower, and gum never replaces a toothbrush. Ensuring that your body and your clothes are clean goes a long way.

ENGAGED: No, I am not talking about him putting a ring on it. I am referring to your level of engagement on the date and during your interactions with him. Being attentive and engaged communicates interest. Additionally, being mentally present puts you in a space to have a fair and honest assessment of him and of you with him. Plan to limit your distractions when speaking with him on the phone and during an actual date.

> *Refrain from excessive phone usage*: Excessive phone usage could occur if you answer non-emergency text messages and phone calls from family or friends (this excludes the designated safety friend) or if you check work emails during your date or if you are continuously checking or posting on social media. Any one of these behaviors can signal disinterest, immaturity, and/or cluelessness.

> *Beware of overly involved conversations with others:* The people at the next table might be extremely friendly or the barista might have on the nicest shade of lipstick or the person behind you looks so familiar. But now is not the time to have friendly chitchat with any of them.

Being too focused on yourself: Whether you are nervous and self-conscious or overconfident bordering on self-absorbed, thinking about yourself excessively can be a huge turnoff. Leave space in the conversation for both you and him. Leave your compact mirror in your purse and fight the urge to check your lipstick, your bangs, and your eye shadow. Rest assured that you will remain as cute as you were when you left the house throughout the duration of the date.

GROUNDED: Being your best self includes being grounded. This might be a new idea for some of you, but it might be one of the most important traits that you work to develop. When we think of a person who is grounded, we think of certain characteristics that radiate from them. Being grounded is a state of being versus taking specific action. Grounded individuals possess a state of calm and centeredness that leaves them virtually unshakeable. They are able to maintain their composure in the face of the unpredictable. They are solid in who they are and in their ability to handle situations as they arise. Grounded individuals have learned ways to manage emotions such as anxiety, fear, and worry to remain cool, calm, and collected. They are rooted in the present moment and strive for balance.

If you have difficulty remaining grounded, these two practices might help you to develop in this area.

1. **Take deep breaths:** Have you ever watched a newborn baby breathe? If not, pay attention the next time one is in close proximity. Newborns don't breathe from their chest; they breathe from their diaphragm. The diaphragm is an organ that sits underneath the bottom of the rib cage on top of the stomach. When newborns breathe, their little tummies rise and fall with each breath, not their chests. They take long, deep breaths that flow through their entire upper torso. For some reason, as we get older, we forget how to breathe, and our breaths become more and more shallow. We mindlessly take shallow, short breaths that barely fill our lungs to capacity. However, purposefully taking long, slow breaths that fill our lungs

and our diaphragm actually helps to produce a state of calm, relaxation, and focus. Practice breathing in through your nose for a count of seven and out through your mouth for a count of ten throughout the day (ensuring that your stomach rises and falls). Pay attention to your breathing and the sensations in your body. Try to do this whenever you feel anxious, to help you relax and stay in the moment.

2. **Develop an internal fan:** Interestingly, most of us don't have to intentionally develop an inner critic: that inside voice that judges, criticizes, catastrophizes, points out mistakes, and questions all decisions. Somehow the inner critic just magically shows up when we are old enough to recognize it. However, most of us do have to intentionally develop an internal fan: that inside vocal supporter that comforts, encourages, uplifts, gives grace, reminds us of our strengths, and tells us that all will be OK. Development of the internal fan must be deliberate and a daily practice. The internal fan develops when we consciously practice positive self-talk to help quiet the inner critic. Positive self-talk does not need to consist of long, intense monologues refuting negative thoughts that pop into your head. The kind things that we say to ourselves can be brief statements that remind us of who we are. Saying things to yourself like "You're OK," "You can do it," "You are brave," "It's not the end of the world," "You got this," et cetera, can go a long way in helping you to remain grounded and present. Create your own brief affirmations to say to yourself throughout the days.

Chapter 7 serves as a reminder that if you keep doing the same thing, you will continue to get the same results. In order to increase our dating potential, we must face our fears and encourage ourselves to get out of our comfort zone. Given the limited free time that most women have these days, we must be strategic in our planning. Where will you go? Which friend will you go with? What new things will you try? The answers to these questions cannot be left to happenstance. Additionally, when you get there, you must be your best self. Now it is time to take that step.

Chapter 7 Reflection

What did I learn about myself in this chapter?

_____

_____

_____

_____

_____

_____

_____

_____

_____

_____

_____

_____

_____

_____

_____

_____

_____

_____

_____

_____

_____

_____

_____

🦋 What did I learn about my dating habits in this chapter?

_____

_____

_____

_____

_____

_____

_____

_____

_____

_____

_____

_____

🦋 What do I want to change about my past dating behavior?

_____

_____

_____

_____

_____

_____

_____

_____

_____

_____

_____

_____

_____

_____

🦋 What skills and tools did I learn in this chapter?

_____
_____
_____
_____
_____
_____
_____
_____
_____
_____

🦋 What will I do to date differently?

_____
_____
_____
_____
_____
_____
_____
_____
_____
_____
_____
_____
_____
_____

8

After the Date

Dating has taught me what I want and don't want,
who I am, and who I want to be.

—*Jennifer Love Hewitt*

Here you are at chapter 8. This chapter cannot be completed until you have gone on your first date. This entire chapter is devoted to helping you to evaluate your date, the dating experience itself, and to determine next steps.

You've done a lot of work in preparation for this part. It is time to go back, review your responses, and put what you have discovered into action. Return to this page after your first date.

Congratulations, you have gone out on your first date since completing the book. However, your work is not complete. This next phase will require that you review some of the work you have done in previous chapters and apply it to your post-date deliberations. Now is the time to sit down and reflect on both your thoughts and feelings about the date. In this chapter you are not reflecting on whether he is the "one," but more simply you are just evaluating whether you would want another date.

DATE EVALUATION

You are to complete these two exercises after each date that you have. If you go out with the same guy more than once, you are to complete these exercises after each of the first three dates.

Remember that the goal is for you to use both your head and your heart to determine if this date was in line with your purpose and whether it deserves more of your time.

Return to chapter 5 and copy your Essentials. Use these to reflect on your date. Check the column to the right that indicates whether he possessed your Essentials. Then do the same for the list of "prefilled" descriptions below that. Did he exhibit any of these seven red-flag traits?

CAPACITY TRAITS: QUICK ONCE-OVER (APPENDIX 8)

ESSENTIALS	Y	N	?
1.			
2.			
3.			
4.			
5.			
6.			
7.			
8.			
9.			
10.			
RED FLAGS	**Y**	**N**	**?**
1. Neediness			
2. Control/Domination			
3. Negative/Critical			
4. Entitlement/Selfish			
5. Performer/All About Me			
6. Closed Off/Evasive			
7. Victimization			

🦋 Does he currently possess my Essentials?

_____

_____

_____

_____

_____

_____

_____

_____

🦋 How has he demonstrated the capacity to possess my Essentials?

_____

_____

_____

_____

_____

_____

_____

_____

_____

_____

_____

🦋 What red flags, if any, has he demonstrated?

_____

_____

_____

_____

_____

_____

_____

_____

_____

_____

_____

THE DATED EVALUATION FORM

The DATED evaluation form (appendix 9) should be used after each new date and for the first three dates (if he makes it past the first date). This form should be completed within two hours of the end of the date. This will allow for you to provide answers while the date is still fresh in your mind.

DATED Evaluation Form (Sample)

D—Describe when (date, time), who (name and demographics), where and what (initial feelings and thoughts that came up)

> *Jackson Brown, 39 years old, delivery driver, divorced, no kids but wants them. Lunch date at La Petite Tea and Biscuit House. Pretty nice looking, clothes were clean, and he smelled fresh, seemed nice enough, he was a bit nervous at first but conversation flowed.*

A—All good (Essentials)

> *He was easy to talk to. He wants kids and so do I. He says that family is very important to him. He has a steady job and owns a condo. He was polite to the hostess and waited until my food arrived before he ate. He has a great sense of humor. His five-year plan is to buy his own delivery trucks to start his own company.*

T—Trouble (red flags)

> *Says that family is most important, but he hasn't spoken to his brother or sister in over a year. Also wants to start his own delivery business but not sure if he has a plan—must evaluate capacity vs. potential. Chews with his mouth open.*

◄▌ *E*—Evaluation (overall impressions)

If your friend told you about this guy and their first date, this would be your feedback/response.

If my friend told me about Jackson, I'd tell her that he sounds lukewarm. Doesn't sound like she's really into him. Maybe she should go out with him once more and see if there is any chemistry, but if not, time to move on.

◄▌ *D*—Determinations (prognosis: good, fair, poor)

The prognosis is fair at this point because it can go either way. I will agree to one more lunch date (hopefully in the next week), and I will further assess the red flags that I saw and see if I am more attracted to him.

DATED EVALUATION FORM (APPENDIX 9)

◄▌ *D*—Describe when (date, time), who (name and demographics), where and what (initial feelings and thoughts that came up)

_____

_____

_____

_____

_____

_____

_____

_____

_____

A—All good (Essentials)

_____

_____

_____

_____

_____

T—Trouble (red flags)

_____

_____

_____

_____

_____

E—Evaluation (overall impressions)

If your friend told you about this guy and their first date, this would be your feedback/response.

_____

_____

_____

_____

_____

D—Determinations (prognosis: good, fair, poor)

_____

_____

_____

_____

_____

_____

HOW TO BOW OUT GRACEFULLY

It is wonderful when things go great. But what happens when things don't go so well? What happens when you decide that "he" is not right and you are ready to move on? How do you do this? What do you say? When do you say it?

Leaving a budding relationship can be just as difficult as getting into one. As was discussed in chapter 1, there are many reasons that we stay longer than we should. Hopefully, deciding very early on will make this process easier. It should be easier to walk away after three dates than it is after two years.

Five Tips on Bowing Out Gracefully

1. Be sure.

   The most important step to bowing out gracefully is for you to be sure that you are not interested in pursuing anything further with him. Bowing out should not be done on impulse or as an emotional response. It is crucial for you to have reflected on your decision, determined why you need to move on, and to be certain that this is the best thing for you at this time. Once you are firm in your decision, you need to move forward as quickly as possible.

2. Develop a plan.

   The what, how, and when should be dependent on the nature of the relationship that you've had. The length of time and the level of intensity with which you have dated should inform the way you end the involvement.

   What: What will you say? Be kind and have a positive tone. If he becomes angry or emotionally volatile, leave the conversation immediately. If they go low, you go high.

How: How will this conversation take place? Generally, I would not suggest that having such a serious conversation by telephone or by text is respectful or acceptable. However, if you have only had one or two dates and have communicated most often using these means, then they are perfectly appropriate. If you do decide to have this conversation in person, I suggest that you have "the talk" in a neutral public location.

When: This conversation should take place within twenty-four to forty-eight hours after you have made the decision to withdraw.

3. Be direct.

    This is not the time to be vague and tentative. Unfortunately, this is one of those situations where ripping the bandage off is better than a slow, steady pull. Let him know that you are not interested in pursuing the relationship any further. This conversation should be more about you than it is about him.

4. Do not offer to remain friends.

    Oftentimes, people offer their friendship as a consolation prize. It makes the breakup seem less "harsh" and reassures him that he's a nice guy. So nice, in fact, that he'd make a great friend. There are several reasons that this is not a good idea in this case: (a) When you are beginning to date, this gesture can send mixed messages. (b) You are dating with purpose, so having a cadre of newfound male friends hanging around can derail your purpose. (c) Spending time with him as a "friend" can create a connection of familiarity and cloud your judgment. And the list can go on.

5. Make it a clean break.

Don't call to check up on him or to ask him one lingering question. Allow him to go on with his life as you move forward with yours.

MY WORK HERE IS DONE

You did it! You set a goal in chapter 1, and you did the work to accomplish it. This workbook has provided you with information and tools that can and will help you date more effectively. Now it is up to you. You must continually reflect on what you've learned about yourself and commit to implementing strategies that are in line with your dating purpose.

As you move forward, remember that the only thing that you can change is you. Remember that you bring yourself into relationships, and that influences the way the relationship begins, develops, and potentially ends or becomes forever. Work on you, and you will see a difference in who you draw and how things turn out!

APPENDIXES

APPENDIX 1

DATING WITH PURPOSE	DATING IN DESPERATION
☐ Interested in finding a long-term relationship	☐ Change your behaviors to get him to like you
☐ Honest about needs and desires	☐ Agree with everything that he says
☐ Direct	☐ Planning your wedding mentally not long after you first meet
☐ Reflect on your role in the relationship	☐ Always available
☐ Emotionally available and stable	☐ Cancel previously made plans when he says he wants to see you
☐ Have identified and communicated dealbreakers	☐ Dig for compliments
☐ Willing to walk away if dealbreakers occur	☐ Need to be told often that he likes you
☐ Well-defined and communicated boundaries	☐ Insecurity
☐ Comfortable saying no	☐ Become anxious if you are unable to answer every time he calls
☐ Comfortable saying yes	☐ Buying gifts and giving money
☐ Dates with both head and heart	☐ Settle/lower your standards so that he fits them
☐ Takes time to get to know him	☐ Wavering boundaries
☐ Not looking for a "project"	☐ Clingy
☐ Ready for commitment	☐ Popping up at his house or job uninvited
☐ Willing to leave unhealthy relationship	☐ You truly believe that a part of a man is better than no man
☐ Comfortable maintaining your identity when in a relationship	☐ You tell him sad stories to make it more difficult for him to leave you
☐ OK with taking it slow	☐ Justify his rude, disrespectful, or bad behavior
☐ Comfortable allowing him to be him and you to be you	☐ Send long, emotional text messages
☐ Not willing to settle	☐ Become upset when he is unavailable
☐ Not emotionally reactive	☐ Use sex to "help" him commit to the relationship
☐ Are clear about why you are dating	☐ Believe that if you have sex with him, he will stay
☐ Outline those things that you are looking for in a mate	☐ Believe that if you have a child with him, he will stay

APPENDIX 2

	CHARACTERISTICS OF HEALTHY RELATIONSHIPS		
☐ Y N	Mutual trust	☐ Y N	Similar values
☐ Y N	Mutual respect	☐ Y N	Willingness to be vulnerable
☐ Y N	Have fun together	☐ Y N	Accept the other as he/she is
☐ Y N	Physical affection	☐ Y N	Similar goals
☐ Y N	Neither partner tries to "fix" the other	☐ Y N	Have separate interests and identities
☐ Y N	Treat each other as equals	☐ Y N	Physical attraction
☐ Y N	Free from personal attacks, name-calling, sarcasm, belittling, and humiliation	☐ Y N	Look out for each other's best interests
☐ Y N	Rules and boundaries are respected and honored	☐ Y N	There is a balance of closeness and separation
☐ Y N	Fight fair	☐ Y N	Shared power
☐ Y N	Opinions are valued	☐ Y N	Ability to maintain sense of self
☐ Y N	Each person feels responsible for their own happiness and well-being	☐ Y N	Support and encourage each other
☐ Y N	You feel physically safe, and your partner doesn't force you to have sex or to do things that make you feel uncomfortable.	☐ Y N	Openness to recognizing when the relationship is changing.
☐ Y N	Each partner feels whole without the other	☐ Y N	Rules and boundaries are clear
☐ Y N	Communication is open and respectful	☐ Y N	Each partner is able to regulate their emotions
☐ Y N	Needs and expectations are clearly articulated	☐ Y N	Consistent displays of fondness and admiration

APPENDIX 3

VALUES LIST		
Abundance	Curiosity	Maturity
Acceptance	Daring	Meaning
Accomplishment	Decisiveness	Mindfulness
Adaptability	Discipline	Nonconformity
Affection (loving and caring)	Empathy	Obedience
Altruism	Enthusiasm	Open-mindedness
Ambition	Fairness	Optimism
Assertiveness	Family	Passion
Assurance	Fearlessness	Peace
Audacity	Fidelity	Power
Awareness	Flexibility	Practicality
Beauty	Freedom	Rationality
Brilliance	Friendship	Realism
Certainty	Frugality	Reflection
Challenge	Fun	Reliability
Change	Generosity	Reputation
Clarity	Gratitude	Resilience
Commitment	Growth	Resourcefulness
Community	Health	Respect
Compassion	Honesty	Responsibility
Confidence	Imagination	Security
Conformity	Independence	Self-control
Congruency	Individuality	Selflessness
Connection	Influence	Self-reliance
Consciousness	Integrity	Self-respect
Consistency	Intellect	Sensitivity
Control	Intimacy	Sensuality
Conviction	Introspection	Strength
Courage	Intuition	Trust
Creativity	Justice	Truth
Credibility	Kindness	Unity
	Loyalty	Warmth

APPENDIX 4

VIOLENCE

PHYSICAL SEXUAL

USING COERCION AND THREATS
Making and/or carrying out threats to do something to hurt her • threatening to leave her, to commit suicide, to report her to welfare • making her drop charges • making her do illegal things.

USING INTIMIDATION
Making her afraid by using looks, actions, gestures • smashing things • destroying her property • abusing pets • displaying weapons.

USING ECONOMIC ABUSE
Preventing her from getting or keeping a job • making her ask for money • giving her an allowance • taking her money • not letting her know about or have access to family income.

USING EMOTIONAL ABUSE
Putting her down • making her feel bad about herself • calling her names • making her think she's crazy • playing mind games • humiliating her • making her feel guilty.

POWER AND CONTROL

USING MALE PRIVILEGE
Treating her like a servant • making all the big decisions • acting like the "master of the castle" • being the one to define men's and women's roles

USING ISOLATION
Controlling what she does, who she sees and talks to, what she reads, where she goes • limiting her outside involvement • using jealousy to justify actions.

USING CHILDREN
Making her feel guilty about the children • using the children to relay messages • using visitation to harass her • threatening to take the children away.

MINIMIZING, DENYING AND BLAMING
Making light of the abuse and not taking her concerns about it seriously • saying the abuse didn't happen • shifting responsibility for abusive behavior • saying she caused it.

PHYSICAL SEXUAL

VIOLENCE

Source: www.theduluthmodel.org

APPENDIX 5

FOUR-SQUARE PLAN

ESSENTIALS (VALUES)	DEALBREAKERS (BOUNDARIES)
(example: must want children)	*(example: verbal, physical, or emotional abuse)*

NEGOTIABLES (COMPROMISES)	DOESN'T MATTER (UNIMPORTANT)
(example: relocation)	*(example: college degree)*

APPENDIX 6

SAFETY CHECKLIST AND PLAN

TASK	DETAILS	✓
1. Social media account privacy setting		
2. Online screen name		
3. Internet search (him)		
4. Internet search (me)		
5. How will I get there?		
6. First-date places		
7. Friends I will notify about my dates		
8. When will I tell him that I've taken these precautions?		
9. This friend will call while I'm on the date:		
10. My nonalcoholic beverages will be:		
11. How will I ensure that my food/drink is not left unattended?		
12. Days of the week that are usually good for (lunch) dates		
13. I commit to leaving if I become uncomfortable.		
14. Make sure I have: Money Cell phone Pepper spray Key-chain alarm		
15. I have done steps 1 through 14.		

APPENDIX 7

RED FLAG CHECKLIST	✓
1. Does he seem too good to be true?	❑
2. Does he say, "Let's be friends first" but doesn't respect personal space and sexual boundaries?	❑
3. Does he send sexual or nude pictures or ask for them?	❑
4. Does he have an addiction, whether substance (alcohol, drugs) or behavior (gambling, porn), that he refuses to get help for because "it is not a problem"?	❑
5. Is he married or otherwise unavailable to be in a committed relationship right now?	❑
6. Does he no-show for dates?	❑
7. Does he talk about his past relationships a lot?	❑
8. Does conversation often revolve around him (what he's doing, what he needs, what he likes, what he wants, what he thinks, etc.)?	❑
9. Is he standoffish, shallow, or emotionally distant?	❑
10. Is his behavior inconsistent or changing often?	❑
11. Is he rude or disrespectful toward you or others?	❑
12. Does he lack integrity in dealing with things (honesty, money) or people?	❑
13. Does he have a quick fuse and react to frustration with extreme anger or blame?	❑
14. Does he have difficulty accepting responsibility? Is it always someone else's fault?	❑
15. Is his life unstable or filled with drama or things that need to be "worked out" (whether it's his fault or not)?	❑
Add your own:	
16.	
17.	❑
	❑

APPENDIX 8

CAPACITY TRAITS: QUICK ONCE-OVER

ESSENTIALS	Y	N	?
1.			
2.			
3.			
4.			
5.			
6.			
7.			
8.			
9.			
10.			
RED FLAGS	**Y**	**N**	**?**
1. Neediness			
2. Control/Domination			
3. Negative/Critical			
4. Entitlement/Selfish			
5. Performer/All About Me			
6. Closed Off/Evasive			
7. Victimization			

APPENDIX 9

DATED EVALUATION FORM

D—Describe when (date, time), who (name and demographics), where and what (initial feelings and thoughts that came up)

_____

_____

_____

A—All good (Essentials)

_____

_____

_____

T—Trouble (red flags)

_____

_____

_____

E—Evaluation (overall impressions)
If your friend told you about this guy and their first date, this would be your feedback/ response.

_____

_____

_____

D—Determinations (prognosis: good, fair, poor)

_____

_____

_____

ACKNOWLEDGMENTS

Thank you to my husband, ADG, for your unconstrained love and support and for being my first Dating with Purpose case study. You have proven that "they" do exist and that forever can be a reality.

Thank you to my son, Jace, for so selflessly sharing me with the world. If I were taken back in time and shown all the available babies in the whole entire world, I would choose you always! Thank you to my wedding present, Kendelle: you are a very special young lady, and I feel honored to be with you on this journey called life.

I want to thank my big brother, Vincent, for always paving the way and for always reminding me that "it" is possible. Thank you to my baby brother, Ural, for living with no limits and showing me the value in going for "it."

Thank you to the other Graveses—Lisa, Dorothy, and Flimmie (RIH)—for loving me as your own, for encouraging my dreams, and for raising him well.

I would like to thank my former classmates, current colleagues and CSPP-LA Ujima members; you've had considerable influence on my development as a psychologist and a friend. Your wisdom, insight, and wit are with me every step of the way. I love ya'll.

Thank you to Drs. RBK, Kumea, Polite (RIH), and Parks for your professional guidance and personal support. Your training, teaching, mentoring, and belief in me have provided me with an unwavering foundation upon which my professional career is securely anchored.

Thank you to my colleagues, staff, and former trainees at Champion Counseling Center. This would not be possible without the work that you do, the support that you give, the knowledge that you share, and the dedication that you all demonstrate. Thank you for always making me look good.

Thank you to my big ole country family and my California friends, who are too numerous to name, for your warm hugs, available shoulders, and supportive words. Thank you for being my village.

Most importantly, thank God for entrusting me with this vision and purpose.

ABOUT THE AUTHOR

Erica Holmes, PsyD, is core faculty and director of the Psychological Trauma Studies Specialization in the master's in psychology program at Antioch University Los Angeles; executive director of Champion Counseling Center; and the founder of HOMMs Consulting. Since 2001, Dr. Holmes has provided psychotherapy and counseling, training and consultation, and education and research services to individuals and organizations.

Dr. Holmes is a frequent invited speaker at local, national, and international conferences and events. Her areas of inquiry and more than 150 presentations focus on relationships and coupling, insight and empowerment, psychological trauma, psychotherapy with African American clients, and the integration of Christianity and psychology.

She holds a bachelor of science degree in sociology with a minor in behavioral science from California State University, Dominguez Hills, as well as a master's degree and doctorate in clinical psychology from the California School of Professional Psychology. Dr. Holmes also holds postgraduate certifications in the psychology of trauma from Antioch University and in diversity and inclusion from Cornell University. She is an American Psychological Association Minority Fellow and past board member for the Los Angeles chapter of the Association of Black Psychologists.

Made in the USA
Las Vegas, NV
30 January 2022

42629673R00109